The OCCULT ALMANAC

First published in the United Kingdom in 2026 by
Thames & Hudson Ltd, 6–24 Britannia Street, London WC1X 9JD

First published in the United States of America in 2026 by
Thames & Hudson Inc., 500 Fifth Avenue, New York, New York 10110

EU Authorized Representative: Interart S.A.R.L.
19 rue Charles Auray, 93500 Pantin, Paris, France
productsafety@thameshudson.co.uk
www.interart.fr

A CIP catalogue record for this book is available from the British Library.

Library of Congress Control Number 2026934201
ISBN 978-0-500-03151-3
01

Printed in Huizhou, Guangdong, China
TT/June/2026

Conceived, designed and produced by
The Bright Press, an imprint of the Quarto Group,
1 Triptych Place, London SE1 9SH,
United Kingdom.
T (0)20 7700 9000
www.Quarto.com

Publisher: James Evans
Editorial Director: Isheeta Mustafi
Art Director: Emily Nazer
Managing Editor: Lucy Tipton
Commissioning Editor: Caroline Elliker
Senior Editor: Joanna Bentley
Project Editor: Robin Pridy
Design: JC Lanaway
Illustrations: Daisy Webster
Picture Research: Jane Lanaway
Production Manager: Nathan Miller
Consultant: Danny Scopelliti, The Occult Library, occultlibrary.org

FSC
www.fsc.org
MIX
Paper | Supporting responsible forestry
FSC® C016973

The OCCULT ALMANAC

A YEAR OF ESOTERIC EVENTS, SACRED TRADITIONS AND SECRET LORE

LIZ WILLIAMS

T&H

CONTENTS

INTRODUCTION

The almanac is a form of annotated calendar, a guide to the year's months and seasons, and to the stars, plants, gemstones, rites and traditions to which they are tethered. Found across cultures throughout the world, almanacs date from very ancient times, and many aspects of religions and occult practices are attached to them. Some of the best-known almanacs, including *The Old Farmer's Almanac* in the USA and the Huangli in China, are still in production today.

Almanacs can be a balm to the year, helping to ground ourselves in time, with a plethora of practical and magical information, from planetary and astrological data to key festivals, sabbats and rites for each season.

In whatever form they take, almanacs are an integral part of the year for many magical practitioners, or for those who simply want a guide to the phases of the Moon, the zodiac, or the gemstones, plants and trees associated with each month.

Detail from *Saul and the Witch of Endor* by Jacob Cornelisz van Oostsanen, 1526.

A HISTORY OF ALMANACS

Almanacs have long been a staple of folk culture throughout the world. In the UK, *Old Moore's Almanack* was first published in 1697 and continues today, with claims to have predicted the September 11 attacks in the USA. *The Old Farmer's Almanac* (published from 1792) is North America's oldest continuously published periodical, and still offers information about the weather, gardening and the phases of the Moon.

ANCIENT TIES

As far back as the seventh century BCE in Babylon, cuneiform tablets contained astrological data and weather reports. There were also Egyptian almanacs, originally lunar, which evolved into a 365-day civic calendar based on the three seasons of Inundation, Emergence and Harvest. Similarly, China had the Huangli, with information on weather and planting. In India, Panchangam – lunisolar almanacs from possibly the first century BCE – continue. These contain auspicious timings for events, planetary positions and astronomical phenomena. The Ancient Greeks and Romans had calendars detailing festival days, while Ptolemy (100–170 BCE) created the *Tetrabiblos*, an astrological treatise to be used alongside a calendar.

The *Almanac of Azarqueil* was produced in 1088, and Zij tables that predicted celestial phenomena were commonplace in the medieval Islamic world. In Japan, Rokuyō – a medieval six-day calendar – continues to work out people's lucky days. The Aztecs, too, consulted Tonalpohualli, a 260-day ritual calendar with possible origins in the first century BCE. It attributed a deity to each day and contained timings for rituals, ceremonies and practical matters, such as the best day on which to return from a trade expedition. Almanacs produced by the ecclesiastic establishment in medieval Britain included lists of the planetary hours as well as saints' days. Talismans, mention of herbs and advice for divination sometimes appeared in their marginalia.

TOWARDS A MORE MODERN ALMANAC

By the fifteenth century, the emergence of the printing press led to wider almanac use. Astronomer Johannes Kepler paid his bills by drawing up horoscopes for well-known people, but he also produced astrological almanacs for several decades. Despite being known as 'the sceptical astrologer', he strove to reconcile astrology and astronomy.

The first book printed in the American colonies was an almanac, in 1639 – along with dates and astronomical phenomena, it included prophecies. In 1662 in England, *Poor Robin's Almanack* was brought out, probably by William Winstanley. Unlike other almanacs, its purpose was primarily satirical.

The English astrologer John Partridge produced an almanac in the 1700s, which was a characteristic combination of predictions and astrology. Partridge sought to reform astrology by returning to Ptolemaic principles, but he had his detractors: Jonathan Swift himself wrote a fake eulogy for him (see right).

Benjamin Franklin even produced an almanac for several years, as 'Poor Richard' – it was a calendar, combined with seasonal sayings, astronomical and astrological information, and Franklin's own witty proverbs.

Here five foot deep
lyes on his back
A cobbler,
starmonger,
and quack...
Who to the stars
in pure good-will,
Does to his best look
upward still.
Weep all you
customers that use
His pills, his
almanacks or shoes.

—Jonathan Swift

THE MAGICAL YEAR

Many ancient calendars were closely aligned to agricultural cycles, and to the Moon, stars and constellations, weaving in connections to the spiritual and material world to create a 'magical year'.

NOTING CHANGES

Knowing when the harvest should be gathered has been crucial to almost all ancient civilizations, and its importance continues for farmers now. For many, it remains key to know the timings of equinoxes, solstices and various processions of stars across the heavens, since these often herald important events on Earth. For example, the rising of the Dog Star, Sirius, was closely associated with the flooding of the Nile in Ancient Egyptian civilizations. In many cultures, the magical year is more closely aligned to the lunar calendar, as seen in many parts of the Asian continent. It can also be tied to religious or local traditional beliefs, as evident in the 260-day ritual calendar used by the Aztec Empire, or to the Kabbalistic teachings that are linked to Jewish mysticism and astrology (see page 186). Many other cultures base seasonal rites and celebrations around the agricultural year. For example, the festival of Makar Sankranti, held in India and Nepal, marks the end of the winter harvest and involves thanking the sun god as the month moves into Capricorn.

Above: Sirius, also known as the Dog Star, or Sopdet, has long served to mark the transition from high summer to harvest, as well as the Nile's annual flooding in ancient times.

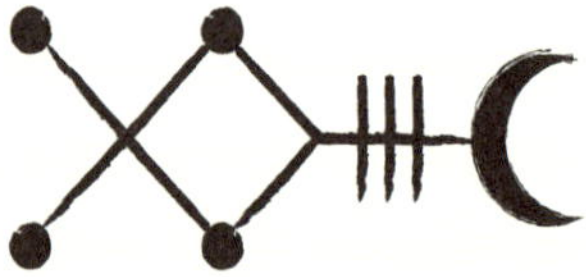

Above: The astrological symbol of Sirius, as noted by writer Heinrich Cornelius Agrippa (1486–1535). He believed the star to be especially useful for magical practice.

CORRESPONDENCES

Understanding magical associations – known as correspondences – guides us into a further understanding of ancient lore and helps us feel part of the weave of the year. These correspondences show how different aspects of the world are connected, and that by working with these systems, power is lent to the spellwork and ritual conducted by the magical practitioner. The range of correspondences is vast, and includes gemstones and Norse runes, Tarot cards, plants and animals, stars, planets and lunar phases as well as supernatural entities such as angels and demons or gods and goddesses – these connect not only to one another but to time itself.

In Renaissance Europe, these systems of correspondence were boosted by herbalists such as Nicholas Culpeper, who included each plant's magical correspondences in his herbals, and by Paracelsus, whose work on the links between the macrocosm (the universe) and the microcosm (humankind) did much to influence magical thought, and found its way into many almanacs and books of magical knowledge, known as grimoires, over the centuries (see below).

Renaissance scholar Paracelsus (1493–1541) believed that divine power was revealed through the relationship between humankind (the microcosm) and the stars (the macrocosm), with each ailment having a cure in nature. His work, *Paragranum*, states the four pillars of medical practice to be natural philosophy, astronomy, alchemy and virtue. Line engraving by T. de Bry, of a Vitruvian man (microcosm) overlaid on the macrocosm, 1617.

CELESTIAL CALENDAR

Time can be structured in many ways, from observing lunar phases to noting constellations or the spaces between them to mark out sections of the year. The Western zodiac, consisting of twelve constellations that start with Aries and end with Pisces, is based on Babylonian and Egyptian astrology, and was further evolved by the Greeks. The Chinese zodiac, based on twelve animals, is probably even older. Some authorities believe that it dates from the Shang Dynasty, 3,000 years ago.

The Inca people identified 'dark' constellations (the spaces between the stars), and their appearance related to agricultural tasks. In Ancient Egypt, the calendar was lunar and each month began when the New Moon was glimpsed. The rising of the Dog Star, Sirius (Sopdet), signified the annual flooding of the Nile; Ancient Egyptian buildings, such as the pyramids, seem to be in alignment with the stars, their constellations associated with gods such as Osiris. Some Islamic cultures today use a lunar (*hijri*) calendar: Saudi Arabia uses one for religious purposes. Vietnam, South Korea and Singapore also use a lunar/solar calendar for religious observances, and the Vedic and Hebrew calendars are lunisolar.

Wiccans hold celebrations known as 'Esbats' on the Full Moon and sometimes on New Moons, while some shamanic peoples hold consultations during the Dark Moon (see opposite).

1. NEW MOON This is the time to start magical projects, and for cleansing and purification. Write down any magical intentions on a piece of paper.

2. WAXING CRESCENT Continue to put intention and energy into any work begun at the New Moon. Practise self-care, ground yourself and strengthen your commitment to your intentions.

3. WAXING HALF MOON Fine-tune your magical intentions and address blocks or obstacles. Rituals for courage and determination are helpful now.

4. WAXING GIBBOUS Time to complete any unfinished magical work before the Full Moon, and do a final ritual of intention-setting.

5. FULL MOON The final period of manifestation for this lunar cycle. Undertake visualizations and purifications (to cleanse negative energies) and release your New Moon magical work into the world: for instance, you can take any written intentions from the New Moon and burn them safely in the Full Moon's light.

6. WANING GIBBOUS This period is for working on what you want to get rid of, to banish or let go of unwanted attachments. It is also a time to express gratitude for the gifts of the Full Moon.

7. WANING HALF MOON
Continue to work on any banishing processes, undertaking visualization and further purification. Work on your intuition, dreams and any shadow work.

8. WANING CRESCENT
This is a time for reflection and rest.

9. DARK MOON This is when the Moon is not visible in the night sky, and occurs between the Waning Crescent and the New Moon for two to three days. Some witches hold that you should not do work at this time, but many feel that this is an ideal period to work with your dreams, with the dark goddesses and gods (Hecate, the Morrigan, aspects of Isis and Osiris, see pages 146 and 170), or on aspects of the subconscious mind. Some practitioners maintain that this is a good time to undertake cursing work.

THE WHEEL OF THE YEAR

In this book, we will be largely referring to the pagan Wheel of the Year, a product of Western Revivalist Paganism, which also follows the Northern Hemisphere's seasons.

The pagan Wheel of the Year is based on eight seasonal festivals, known as sabbats, held at six-week intervals (see opposite). Four of these sabbats are astronomical: the Winter and Summer Solstices (Yule and Litha), and the Spring and Autumn Equinoxes (Ostara and Mabon). The remaining four – Samhain, Imbolc, Beltane and Lughnasadh (or Lammas) – are the 'cross quarter' days, with varied associations and connections – Imbolc in February, for instance, is associated with the goddess Bride and with winter's end.

In contemporary Paganism, Wicca and some aspects of the occult, the Wheel of the Year is based on an agricultural cycle: the goddess gives birth to a sacred child, sometimes known as the Mabon, at Yule. He grows in strength at Imbolc. At the Ostara he reaches adolescence, and at Beltane he becomes the Lover, joining the goddess in her aspect of the Spring Maiden in sexual union. He reaches full maturity at Litha, and is cut down in his aspect of the Corn King at Lughnasadh, in August. He descends into the Underworld at Mabon and becomes the Lord of Shadows at Samhain, until he is reborn as a Lord of Light at Yule once more.

The goddess herself also moves through the year, changing into the Maiden at Imbolc and grows in maturity throughout the year, reaching her full power in the summer and then passing into her phase of the Crone in the autumn and early winter months until she transforms back into the Mother at Yule. Both the goddess and her son thus symbolize the passage of the year: seeds stirring in the heart of winter, emerging as young life in the spring, then maturing throughout the summer until the cutting down period of the harvest and gradual decaying in the autumn.

The Wheel of the Year often maps itself on to other systems, including the Celtic tree calendar that is based on the Irish Ogham alphabet. This names thirteen symbolic trees and their correspondences throughout the year, much like the zodiac (see page 187).

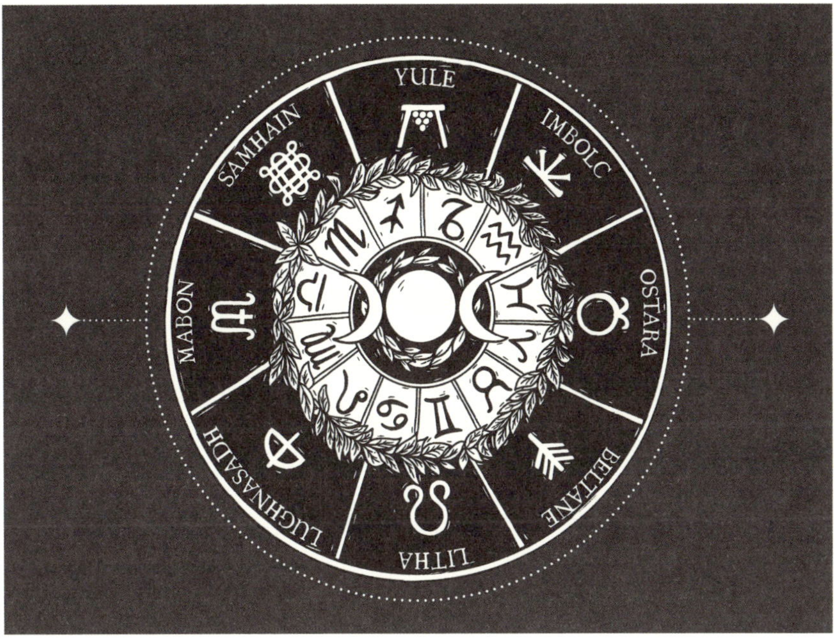

SEASONAL SABBATS

- **Samhain**
  31 Oct–1 Nov
  (see page 149)
- **Yule**
  around 21 December
  (see page 177)
- **Imbolc**
  1 February
  (see page 36)
- **Ostara**
  around 21 March
  (see page 51)
- **Beltane**
  1 May
  (see page 78)
- **Litha**
  around 21 June
  (see page 92)
- **Lughnasadh**
  1 August
  (see page 120)
- **Mabon**
  around 21 September
  (see page 134)

Above: This wheel represents the Northern Hemisphere's sabbats, alongside the zodiac signs for the year. For the Southern Hemisphere, please reverse your seasonal references. For example, it is the Spring Equinox for those above the equator and the Autumn Equinox for those below it.

Left: The Maiden, the Mother and the Crone, seen in the Triple Goddess symbol as phases of the Waxing, Full and Waning Moon.

HOW TO USE THIS BOOK

This almanac is arranged chronologically, so you can turn to the relevant month and discover the many associations that are related to it. It has been presented in the following categories:

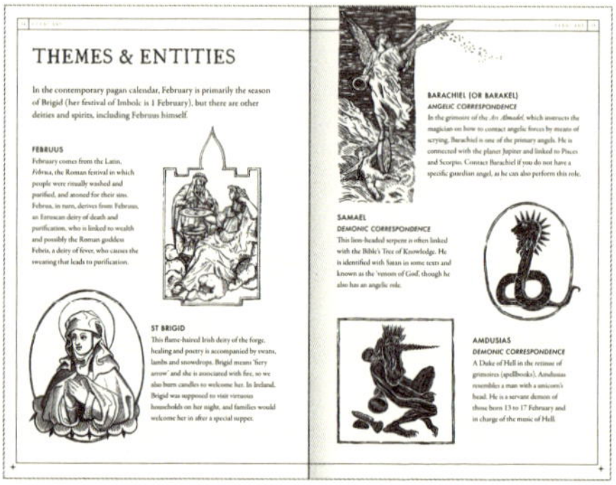

THEMES & ENTITIES

Information on gods, goddesses and supernatural entities, including each month's correspondences to particular angels and demons.

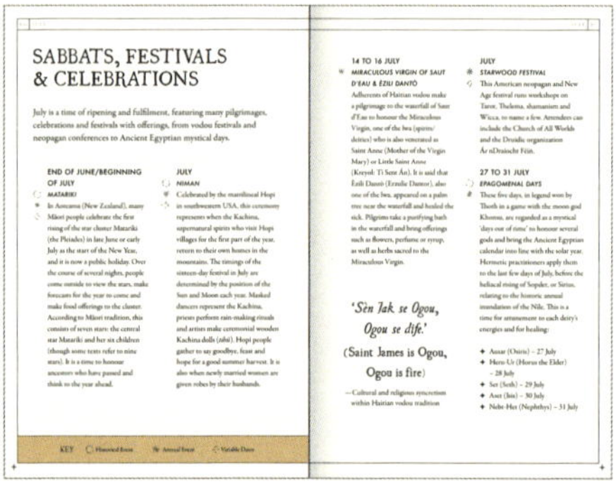

SABBATS, FESTIVALS & CELEBRATIONS

The month's key seasonal, magical and astrological gatherings and festivals around the world.

RITUALS, SPELLS & DIVINATION

Practical spellwork, rites and intentions pertinent to the month's correspondences and themes, alongside divination practices such as numerology, Tarot and Kabbalistic pathworking.

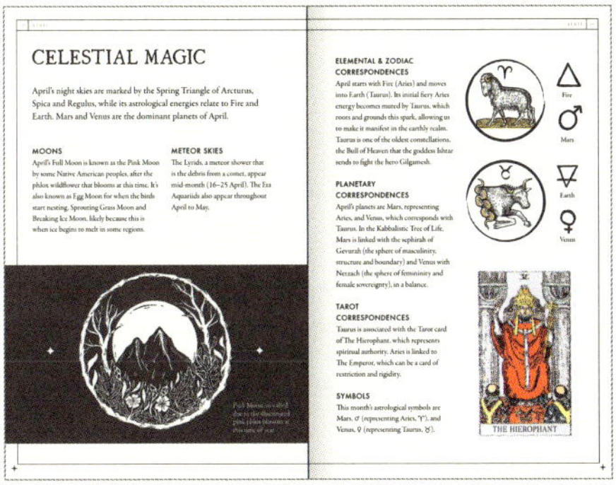

CELESTIAL MAGIC

Constellations, Full Moons, meteor showers, and zodiac and elemental correspondences for the month, along with astrological symbols and planetary, Kabbalistic and Tarot correspondences.

EARTHLY CONNECTIONS

The month's key trees, flowers, herbs, gemstones and runes (symbols from a divinatory system related to Norse mythology).

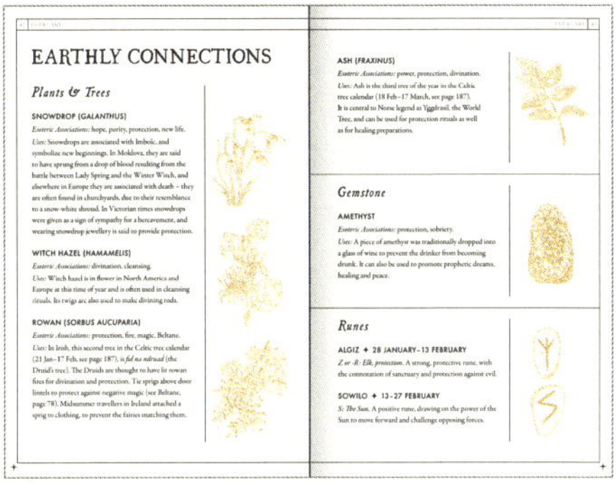

FOLKLORE & MYTH

Unique and important traditions, practices and beliefs for the month, from around the world.

The Divination Directory at the back of the book provides additional information on the magical practices and tools found throughout. Of course, there are far more customs, correspondences and traditions, but we hope that this almanac will provide you with a helpful platform for further exploration.

I

JANUARY

January marks a time of fresh starts and new resolutions. After the social whirl and spiritual significance of the various December festivals, it is a calmer month, with rituals and celebrations that lend light and life to this long dark period of the year. This is a time of purification, blessing and introspective work.

THEMES & ENTITIES

January is named after the two-faced Roman god Janus, who looks both into the past and to the future. In this new year, we too can contemplate the previous year as well as start looking ahead. Spiritually, it's a time of refreshing and cleansing, and of getting one's house in order.

JANUS

Janus also reigns over war and peace: the gates of his temple in Rome were opened when war was declared and closed once peace was re-established. Sometimes acknowledged as a symbolic gatekeeper between different astral worlds or states of consciousness, he is also a god of Time – like Saturn, one of the planetary rulers of this month.

EA

Capricorn the sea-goat appears in Babylonian mythology as Ea (Enki in Sumerian), humankind's benevolent protector, who warns the wise man Utnapishtim of a deluge, caused by the god Enlil. Like Noah, Utnapishtim builds a boat for his relations, tribespeople and young animals, and together they survive.

AMALTHEA/AMALTHEIA

The wet nurse of the Greek god Zeus, Amalthea is linked with the zodiac sign Capricorn and is still acknowledged today in some forms of Hellenic Revivalist Paganism (derived from Ancient Greek mythology and beliefs). She cares for Zeus when his mother, Rhea, hides him from his murderous father Cronus – Old Father Time. In some legends, Amalthea has the child fed by a goat; in others, she is the goat herself.

ARCHANGEL GABRIEL

ANGELIC CORRESPONDENCE

Gabriel assists with communication. With his help, it is believed that we can voice what we truly need.

BIFRONS

DEMONIC CORRESPONDENCE

Bifrons's name means 'two-faced' in Latin, suggesting that he is a corrupted form of Janus.

SABBATS, FESTIVALS & CELEBRATIONS

Although technically starting on the last day of December, New Year's Eve typically sees celebrations go late into the night, through to the first minutes and morning of January. We then move towards Epiphany and Twelfth Night, and to India and Nepal's Makar Sankranti along with the Gambian masquerade of Janjanbureh Kankurang.

31 DECEMBER TO 1 JANUARY

○ *NEW YEAR'S EVE*

✱ This global celebration often features a night of street parties and fireworks, along with regional customs (see page 30). Northern England and Scotland celebrate Hogmanay and first-foooting (welcoming the first person, historically a tall, dark-haired man, through the front door after midnight on New Year's Eve). Viking-inspired Up Helly Aa in the Shetland Islands marks the end of Yule (see page 177) with torch-lit processions, costumed revellers and the burning of a replica Viking ship.

5 OR 6 JANUARY

○ *TWELFTH NIGHT & EPIPHANY*

✱ ◇ Some pagans observe Twelfth Night, as it is one of the nights of the year on which the Wild Hunt is said to ride, led by Herne, a form of the Horned God in Wicca. Epiphany also has significance in European witchcraft and folk magic, and is a time for divination and blessing the house. In some parts of Europe, the door is 'chalked' – inscribed with the initials of the Three Kings (Caspar, Melchior and Balthazar) plus crosses and the date, for protective magic, i.e.: '20 ✝ C ✝ M ✝ B ✝ 26'. Epiphany water is said to have powers of blessing and can cleanse the home.

KEY ○ Historical Event ✱ Annual Event ◇ Variable Dates

5 TO 17 JANUARY

WASSAILING

This UK tradition typically occurs on Twelfth Night, when wassailers knock on doors, singing, making noise and offering householders a drink from the communal 'wassail' bowl, which often contains warm, spiced cider, in exchange for a gift or money. In orchard wassailing (typically held on 17 January, or Old Twelfth Night), people visit orchards, sing, drink and thank the trees for their bounty. Probably a Saxon custom, it occurs in areas in England specializing in apple and pear orchards, such as Somerset, Gloucestershire and Herefordshire.

14 OR 15 JANUARY

MAKAR SANKRANTI

Celebrating the harvesting of winter crops, this festival in India and Nepal marks the Sun's entry into Capricorn (Makara) and the gradual return of the light after the period of the Winter Solstice. People fly kites, light bonfires and hold feasts, and may make pilgrimages to rivers in which they ritually bathe.

19 TO 20 JANUARY

SAN SEBASTIAN

This festival, held in Cusco, Peru, honours the Spanish martyr of the same name, who is claimed to have cured the city of the plague and become its patron saint. He is also known as the patron saint of archers and soldiers. The Eve of St Sebastian is marked by vespers (a service of evening prayer), while the following day, a procession of sixty men carries a large platform with the saint's statue through the streets. There are local dances, ritual foods such as *chiri uchu* (an Andean dish eaten cold and containing meat, black mint and seaweed) and drinks such as *chicha de jora* (fermented corn beer).

LATE JANUARY

JANJANBUREH KANKURANG

In the Gambia, the masquerade of Janjanbureh Kankurang begins – a tradition linked to Mandinka rites of passage and initiation into manhood that are held later in the year.

'Open pathways, but do not wash away your luck.'

—Old English proverb

RITUALS, SPELLS & DIVINATION

CLEANSING & DIVINATION

Undertaking a Tarot spread on New Year's Eve can provide you with insight on your year ahead. You could also perform a rune reading or consult a similar oracle (*I Ching*, for example) to help with questions about your future. January is a time for fresh starts: clean the house, smudge with sage (burning herbs to create a cleansing smoke – see page 189) or wash down the window and door sills with salt water or Epiphany water (see page 22).

In some traditions, cleaning with a besom broom is believed to brush away your luck at this time of the year, so perhaps open doors and windows for a time instead – invite negativity to leave, yet leave open pathways for good luck to enter. As a further house blessing, you can chalk your door with the symbols of the Three Kings (see page 22).

INTENTION SETTING

Write this year's intentions or resolutions down and place them in a jar or box you have cleansed and blessed, perhaps including a charm. You can then look at these intentions again at the end of the year to see how far you have come.

RITES

For good fortune, practise Hatsuhinode, the Japanese tradition of seeing the first sunrise of the New Year – this has its roots in agricultural rites honouring the sun goddess Amaterasu. For blessings from the god of the New Year, Toshigamisama, make tall arrangements of pine and bamboo to place at gates or entrances.

NUMEROLOGY

Associated with January (through Saturn, Capricorn's ruler), number 8 represents success, achievement and material wealth.

CELESTIAL MAGIC

The consort of Janus is sometimes held to be the moon goddess Jana/ Iana, who symbolizes the year's first New Moon, a powerful time for setting intentions. This cold month, often with clear frosty skies, is a good time to observe the stars and the phases of the Moon.

WOLF MOON

The first Full Moon of the year is known as the Wolf Moon: a time when wolves howl in the desolation of midwinter. Use its power magically to strengthen connections with your community.

METEOR SKIES

The Quadrantid meteor shower – most visible in the Northern Hemisphere – peaks in early January, near the Boötes constellation ('the Herdsman').

The constellation of Boötes – shown here as the hunter and his hounds.

ELEMENTAL & ZODIAC CORRESPONDENCES

January's principal element is Earth, associated with the zodiac sign of practical Capricorn, the mer-goat, before shifting into Air and Aquarius (the Water-bearer) later in the month. Capricorn is a creature of both Earth and Water, while Aquarius stands with feet upon the Earth, but balancing Water between two amphorae.

PLANETARY CORRESPONDENCES

Capricorn is ruled by the planet Saturn. In the ancient Judaic system of the Kabbalah, which divides the cosmology into ten divine spheres, or sephiroth, on the Tree of Life (see page 186), Saturn is connected to the sphere of Binah (structure and discipline). Aquarius is ruled by Uranus, also connected to Binah, but may also be linked to Chokmah, the sphere of wisdom.

TAROT CORRESPONDENCES

Capricorn is linked to The Devil card; Aquarius to the Temperance card.

SYMBOLS

January's astrological symbols relate to Capricorn, ♑, and Aquarius, ♒, along with Saturn, ♄, and Uranus, ♅.

EARTHLY CONNECTIONS

Plants & Trees

CARNATION (*DIANTHUS CAROPHYLLUS*)

Esoteric Associations: love, affection, birth, death.

Uses: Said to have sprung from the tears of the Virgin Mary when she witnessed her son's crucifixion, carnations can be used in vodou rituals as a blood alternative, and were used in floral crowns during Ancient Roman rituals.

LAVENDER (*LAVANDULA*)

Esoteric Associations: protection, cleansing, purification.

Uses: Incense can be used for house clearing. Carry a small lavender bag for protection.

PEPPERMINT (*MENTHA X PIPERITA*)

Esoteric Associations: cleansing, clearing.

Uses: Use the oil in a cleansing bath, prior to undertaking any New Year rituals.

CEDAR (*CEDRUS*), JUNIPER (*JUNIPERUS*), PINE (*PINUS*), SANDALWOOD (*SANTALUM*)

Esoteric Associations: new life, winter festivals, cleansing.

Uses: Evergreens are considered sacred to this time of year. Use pine needles (in an oil, or to burn) in spells or rituals to release negative energy and cleanse. Or use a Fire of Azrael (made of cedar wood, juniper and sandalwood), which is said to induce visions and to aid in foreseeing the year ahead.

BIRCH (*BETULA*)

Esoteric Association: new beginnings.

Uses: This first tree in the Celtic tree calendar (24 Dec–20 Jan, see page 187) has links to the Moon, possibly thanks to its silvery bark. Birch twigs are typically used for besom brooms, but do not use them during January, as it is thought to sweep away good luck (see page 25).

Gemstones

GARNET

Esoteric Associations: cleansing, protection.

Uses: January's birthstone is dedicated to strength and passion.

ONYX

Esoteric Associations: longevity, resilience.

Uses: Onyx gives protective, grounding energy to the body and promotes a sense of security.

JASPER

Esoteric Associations: purity, sacred space.

Uses: Jasper is protective and said to promote stability and vitality.

Runes

EIHWAZ ✦ 28 DECEMBER–13 JANUARY

EI: Yew tree. Relates to the cycles of life and death. It can be a strong protector, or a strong banishing force.

PERTHRO ✦ 13–28 JANUARY

P: Perhaps 'pear tree'. This mysterious rune refers to that which is hidden and opaque; linked to notion of 'wyrd'.

FOLKLORE & MYTH

NEW YEAR CUSTOMS

There are many of these, including eating soba noodles in Japan, and throwing furniture out of the window in Italy. Try to make sure that you have a full wallet – an omen of good financial fortune for the year ahead. In Denmark, to ward off evil spirits, some throw plates and glasses against people's front doors. For good luck in Scotland, people traditionally exchange coal, silverware and shortbread.

AÑOS VIEJOS

In some parts of South America on New Year's Eve, effigies of upopular people from the old year (*años viejos*) are set alight to ward off evil spirits as well as to symbolize the passing of the old year and make way for the new.

'If New Year's Eve night wind blow south, It betokeneth warmth and growth.'

—Shepherd's Kalendar, 1908

HUNTING THE WREN

In Wales, between Christmas Day and Twelfth Night, groups of boys would roam about until they found a wren, which they would kill and then carry ceremoniously around the town on a bier. Origins are unclear but on the Isle of Man, it was said that a wicked fairy came to the island, drowned a number of men, then fled in the form of a wren. The custom died out by the 1880s but has been revived – with a replica.

MARI LWYD

This Welsh custom, also taking place between Christmas Day and Twelfth Night, is a kind of guising or mumming: groups of men go from house to house collecting money, accompanied by the Mari Lwyd – the old grey mare, who takes the form of a horse's skull on top of a pole, carried by someone enveloped in a sheet. The group enters into a 'call-and-response' rhyme with the householder, who refuses to let them in (a process known as a *pwnco*). Eventually the householder invites the Mari and her troupe inside for food and drink. On leaving, they bless the household. Today, the Mari Lwyd is often a participant in pagan rituals.

Mari Lwyd: an increasingly popular manifestation of Welsh folklore.

II

FEBRUARY

February, known in Old English as *Solmonath* ('mud month') or *Kale-monath* ('cabbage month'), marks the very first stirrings of spring and the important pagan celebration of Imbolc. Lambing begins and the first shoots of flowers, including the beloved snowdrop with its strong magical correspondences, start to emerge.

THEMES & ENTITIES

In the contemporary pagan calendar, February is primarily the season of Brigid (her festival of Imbolc is 1 February), but there are other deities and spirits, including Februus himself.

FEBRUUS

February comes from the Latin, *Februa*, the Roman festival in which people were ritually washed and purified, and atoned for their sins. Februa, in turn, derives from Februus, an Etruscan deity of death and purification, who is linked to wealth and possibly the Roman goddess Febris, a deity of fever, who causes the sweating that leads to purification.

ST BRIGID

This flame-haired Irish deity of the forge, healing and poetry is accompanied by swans, lambs and snowdrops. Brigid means 'fiery arrow' and she is associated with fire, so we also burn candles to welcome her. In Ireland, Brigid was supposed to visit virtuous households on her night, and families would welcome her in after a special supper.

BARACHIEL (OR BARAKEL)

ANGELIC CORRESPONDENCE

In the grimoire of the *Ars Almadel*, which instructs the magician on how to contact angelic forces by means of scrying, Barachiel is one of the primary angels. He is connected with the planet Jupiter and linked to Pisces and Scorpio. Contact Barachiel if you do not have a specific guardian angel, as he can also perform this role.

SAMAEL

DEMONIC CORRESPONDENCE

This lion-headed serpent is often linked with the Bible's Tree of Knowledge. He is identified with Satan in some texts and known as the 'venom of God', though he also has an angelic role.

AMDUSIAS

DEMONIC CORRESPONDENCE

A Duke of Hell in the retinue of grimoires (spellbooks), Amdusias resembles a man with a unicorn's head. He is a servant demon of those born 13 to 17 February and in charge of the music of Hell.

SABBATS, FESTIVALS & CELEBRATIONS

February festivals include Chinese New Year, which clears the way for good luck, then Imbolc and Candlemas, which celebrate fire and the returning light. Later in the month come the days that celebrate love – St Valentine's Day and its Welsh equivalent, St Dwynwen's Day. Elsewhere in the world, Setsuban-Sai is celebrated in Japan, while some pagans adopt elements of the Ancient Roman Lupercalia.

FIRST NEW MOON BETWEEN 21 JANUARY AND 20 FEBRUARY

○ ***CHINESE NEW YEAR***

✳ ◇ The Chinese zodiac contains twelve animals, each one representing one year in a twelve-year calendar. Each new year celebrates a new animal (2026 is the Year of the Horse) and is closely linked to astrology. Also called the Spring Festival, Chinese New Year celebrations last for two weeks. During this time, people clean their houses to clear the way for good luck, let off firecrackers, give money in red envelopes and enjoy family meals.

1 FEBRUARY

○ ***IMBOLC/CANDLEMAS***

✳ Imbolc is the pagan festival held on 1 February dedicated to the Goddess Bride (Brigid). Its name may come from *i mbolg*, meaning 'in the belly'. The rest of the year is considered to be gestating 'in the belly' of this month. It is also linked to the Christian festival of Candlemas, held on 2 February, which celebrates the presentation of Christ in the Temple at Jerusalem by his parents.

At Imbolc, a typical pagan ceremony will involve the invocation of the four directions to make a sacred circle. Invocations to Bride

KEY ○ Historical Event ✳ Annual Event ◇ Variable Dates

are made: she might be thanked for heralding the end of winter and the beginning of the spring. Participants may make a Bride's Cross out of rushes for an offering, and gifts of bread and milk are made. Snowdrops will be placed on her altar along with candles, and bonfires may be lit to symbolize the goddess's links to forges and smithcraft. Pagans might also start spring cleaning, since purification is one of Imbolc's aspects (see page 38). It is a joyous celebration, but introspective, since this is still a dark time of the year.

*'If Candlemas Day
is bright and clear,
there'll be two
winters in the year.
If Candlemas be
fair and bright,
winter will have
another flight.'*

—Folk saying

2 OR 3 FEBRUARY

SETSUBUN-SAI

This Japanese festival, in which soybeans are thrown at night, marks the start of spring. It derives from the story of a monk who threw roasted beans at *oni* (trolls or demons) to drive them away. The Japanese word for bean, 豆, can also be inscribed as 'devil's eye' (魔目). Some scholars have suggested that the pronunciation is also close to *mametsu* (魔滅), 'to destroy the devil'.

MID-FEBRUARY

PARENTALIA & LUPERCALIA

Parentalia was a Roman festival held from 13 to 21 February, to honour dead family members. It was then extended to apply to all the dead. The Lupercalia was held around 15 February, to honour Romulus and Remus, the founders of Rome. Priests would sacrifice a goat and a dog, then run through the streets whipping celebrants with strips of goat hide. Some pagans adopt elements of the Lupercalia today.

RITUALS, SPELLS & DIVINATION

RITUALS

February is a time of purification. Bring down any greenery that still remains from the Christmas season and cleanse the house – open windows to let in fresh air, and wash the window and door sills with salt water or a vodou floorwash. Use sage to smudge your home or sacred space (see page 189), or make potpourri of lavender, rosemary and sage if it's difficult to light a smudge stick.

To celebrate Imbolc, place a small bowl of snowdrops (see page 42) in a special place, or on your altar if you have one (see page 189), then light white candles. If you carve or make dolls, make a representation of the Goddess Bride (Brigid) to place in a small basket – this is an old Scots custom known as 'Bride's Bed' – to put by the hearth on Imbolc Eve. It is a way of honouring the goddess and bringing good fortune into the home. In the Outer Hebrides, a representation of Bride would be made and decked with shells, primroses, snowdrops and crystals, with a bright crystal above her heart.

LOVE SPELLS

Magical practitioners may choose to undertake love spells at this time of year, although most responsible magical workers will decline to carry out love magic for other people – it is seen in the Western Mystery Tradition (a broad range of spiritual and esoteric beliefs and practices) as a form of manipulation of the free will of another person and thus frowned upon. You may, of course, choose to do a love spell for yourself, focusing on becoming the kind of person whom others will readily love. Elements for your altar are rose quartz, rose petals and incense (see page 70) or oil dedicated to one of the love goddesses, such as Venus or Aphrodite (see page 62).

NUMEROLOGY

The number 4 is associated with February, via Aquarius's ruler Uranus. It represents change, rebellion and unrest, but can also link to stability and discipline. In traditional astrology, Aquarius's ruler is Saturn, which is linked to the number 8.

'The snowdrop,
in purest white arraie,
First rears her hedde
on Candlemas daie.
While the Crocus
hastens to the shrine
Of Primrose lone on
St Valentine.'

—Excerpt from a nineteenth-century English floral calendar

CELESTIAL MAGIC

Many spiritual practitioners treat February as a time of renewal and inner stillness. We can note small signs of returning life, as winter ends and the light is celebrated with purification and the burning of candles.

MOONS

February's Full Moon is known as the Snow Moon. The Dakota, Lakota and Assiniboine peoples of North America refer to it as the Sore Eyes Moon due to the Sun's rays reflecting off snowfall. The Northern Ojibwe call it the Crows Come Back Moon, as the birds begin to return.

METEOR SKIES

The principal meteor showers at this time of year are the alpha Centaurids, which happen around 8 February, and the delta Normids, which occur around 22 February.

Crows Come Back Moon heralds the birds' return from seasonal migrations.

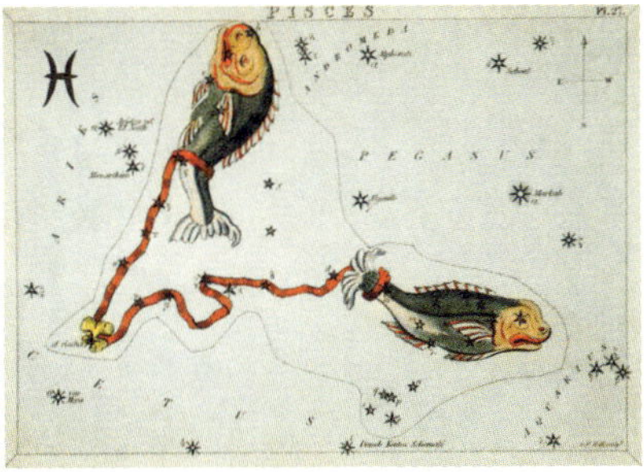

Air

Uranus

Water

Neptune

Jupiter

PLANETARY CORRESPONDENCES

Planets of the month are Uranus, the planet of innovation, radicalism and change, as well as Neptune and Jupiter, which are both connected to Pisces.

TAROT CORRESPONDENCES

Uranus can be linked with The Fool, and has ties to change and uncertainty. The Fool depicts a seeker stepping off a cliff, but ready to trust in what the universe brings. Some also connect the planet to The Tower, as it is the ruler of sudden revolutions.

ELEMENTAL & ZODIAC CORRESPONDENCES

February begins with Air, and the zodiac sign Aquarius, shifting to Water and Pisces later in the month. Air is connected to the mind, thought and intellect, and to spring and dawn while Water links to emotion, love, and to autumn and evening in the Wiccan and other occult systems of correspondence.

SYMBOLS

February's symbols relate to the zodiac signs of Aquarius, ♒, and Pisces, ♓ (the symbol of two fish swimming in different directions can often represent the sign's dual nature). Other symbols include the elements of Air, 🜁, and Water, ▽, the Greek sea god Neptune's trident, ♆, and Uranus, ♅, along with Jupiter, ♃.

EARTHLY CONNECTIONS

Plants & Trees

SNOWDROP (*GALANTHUS*)

Esoteric Associations: hope, purity, protection, new life.

Uses: Snowdrops are associated with Imbolc, and symbolize new beginnings. In Moldova, they are said to have sprung from a drop of blood resulting from the battle between Lady Spring and the Winter Witch, and elsewhere in Europe they are associated with death – they are often found in churchyards, due to their resemblance to a snow-white shroud. In Victorian times snowdrops were given as a sign of sympathy for a bereavement, and wearing snowdrop jewellery is said to provide protection.

WITCH HAZEL (*HAMAMELIS*)

Esoteric Associations: divination, cleansing.

Uses: Witch hazel is in flower in North America and Europe at this time of year and is often used in cleansing rituals. Its twigs are also used to make divining rods.

ROWAN (*SORBUS AUCUPARIA*)

Esoteric Associations: protection, fire, magic, Beltane.

Uses: In Irish, this second tree in the Celtic tree calendar (21 Jan–17 Feb, see page 187), is *fid na ndruad* (the Druid's tree). The Druids are thought to have lit rowan fires for divination and protection. Tie sprigs above door lintels to protect against negative magic (see Beltane, page 78). Midsummer travellers in Ireland attached a sprig to clothing, to prevent the fairies snatching them.

ASH (FRAXINUS)

Esoteric Associations: power, protection, divination.

Uses: Ash is the third tree of the year in the Celtic tree calendar (18 Feb–17 March, see page 187). It is central to Norse legend as Yggdrasil, the World Tree, and can be used for protection rituals as well as for healing preparations.

Gemstone

AMETHYST

Esoteric Associations: protection, sobriety.

Uses: A piece of amethyst was traditionally dropped into a glass of wine to prevent the drinker from becoming drunk. It can also be used to promote prophetic dreams, healing and peace.

Runes

ALGIZ ✦ 28 JANUARY–13 FEBRUARY

Z or -R: Elk, protection. A strong, protective rune, with the connotation of sanctuary and protection against evil.

SOWILO ✦ 13–27 FEBRUARY

S: The Sun. A positive rune, drawing on the power of the Sun to move forward and challenge opposing forces.

FOLKLORE & MYTH

ST VALENTINE'S DAY

Despite the gruesome fate of the original St Valentine (who was flogged, stoned and beheaded on 14 February by Roman Emperor Claudius Gothicus for conducting secret marriages for Christians), his day is now devoted to expressions of love. There are also a number of traditions relating to divination on this day, including divining your future partner through the first bird that you see: for example, if you spot a goldfinch, it is said that you will marry a wealthy man.

DRAGOBETE

In Romanian legend, a beautiful girl named Dochia falls asleep in the mountains and is visited by the god of the mountains in the form of mist. He leaves Dochia pregnant and she gives birth to a boy named Dragobete, who has four godmothers: Autumn, Winter, Spring and Summer. Spring gives him eternal youth, Summer grants him fruitful sweetness, Autumn presents him with a flute and Winter offers shining white clothes. With these gifts, the beautiful Dragobete travels the land seducing the women whom he meets, and appearing on the night of 23 February in the dreams of young women, to instruct them in the ways of love.

'To-morrow is Saint Valentine's day.
All in the morning betime,
And I a maid at your window,
To be your Valentine.'

—Ophelia, in Shakespeare's *Hamlet*

The Eve of St Valentine by George Smith, 1871.

III

MARCH

The first of March heralds the meteorological start of spring, with the Spring Equinox falling around 21 March. The Saxons called the month *Lentmonat*, from which the Christian period of Lent derives. The eighth-century English monk and scholar Bede states that they also named it *Hreth-monath* from the goddess Hretha (though some of the attributions in Bede are of dubious legitimacy).

THEMES & ENTITIES

In contemporary pagan and occult practices, March is a time of awakening and new growth, when the tide of time changes and becomes expansive, allowing growth to occur. March comes from the Latin, *Martius*, signifying the god of war: military campaigns were initiated in spring, along with several festivals of resurrection.

OSTARA

Ostara was adopted by the Brothers Grimm, who cite her as a goddess, and this was taken up by American Wiccan writer Aiden Kelly, who named the Spring Equinox after her. Some believe Ostara to be an old Saxon goddess, though this remains unproven since her first known mention is from Bede, but she is treated as a deity of the spring by many pagans today.

MARS

Though related to the Greek god Ares, Mars is the god of agriculture as well as a deity of military might – unlike Ares, he wields it to bring peace rather than destruction. His consort is Nerio, and he is often linked with Venus, virility and fertility, as well as with protection. The wolf and woodpecker are sacred to him.

ARCHANGEL RAPHAEL

ANGELIC CORRESPONDENCE

Representing spring and the direction of the east, Raphael appears in the ancient *Book of Tobit* as a healer, guide and patron of medical workers and those who travel. He sometimes holds a caduceus, the snake-staff that is a symbol of healing.

MARCHOSIAS

DEMONIC CORRESPONDENCE

In *The Lesser Key of Solomon*, this demon is described as a Marquis of Hell (the name means 'Marquis'), and is depicted as a wolf with fiery breath, the wings of a gryphon and a serpent's tail. He is said to be loyal to the magician who summons him. He is said to hope one day to return to Heaven.

ANGARES

DEMONIC CORRESPONDENCE

Angares appears in various grimoires. He is depicted as an old man riding on a crocodile, or sometimes a cockatrice (a two-legged dragon), with a hawk on his wrist. He is described as being 'under the power of the east' and is thus associated with spring.

SABBATS, FESTIVALS & CELEBRATIONS

March is a time of many festivals worldwide, centring around the Spring Equinox and a returning balance of darkness and light. Pagan celebrations, and Nowruz in the Middle East and Central Asia, all focus on the end of winter and the coming of the spring, celebrated since very ancient times. Easter, too, is a time of rebirth and, like the Jewish Passover, its date is governed by the Moon.

STARTS 9 TO 11 MARCH

◯ ✷ ◇ ***FARVARDIGAN & NOWRUZ (NAVRUZ)***

These Iranian and Kurdish festivals originate in Persia's Zoroastrian religion, and celebrate the Iranian New Year and the coming of spring, when light has victory over the dark of winter. Zoroastrian Parsis in India also celebrate, in March and July/August, and variations have spread to Eastern Europe and many parts of the Asian continent.

During Farvardigan, the ten-day period before Nowruz, people set out food, clean their houses and light a lamp to honour and welcome the souls of the dead. Nowruz has close ties to Rapithwin, a spirit who is both summer and noon, and who returns from his winter's retreat at noonday on Nowruz. The next thirteen days feature dancing, poetry and eating foods made with fresh green herbs as well as rituals such as jumping over bonfires and holding processions and picnics. At Nowruz, seven items are arranged on the Haft-Sin table to represent spring: the *sabzeh*, green, sprouting wheatgrass, sits in the middle of the table, to signify rebirth.

KEY ◯ Historical Event ✷ Annual Event ◇ Variable Dates

AROUND 21 MARCH

SPRING EQUINOX / OSTARA

This is one of the two days in the year (along with the Autumn Equinox, see page 134) when day and night are approximately equal length. Pagans are not the only people who celebrate around this time – the Egyptian festival Sham El Nessim is celebrated as a national holiday on the Monday following Coptic Easter. Its origins stretch back to the time of the pharaohs, when Ancient Egyptians celebrated Shemu, a festival at which people would gather beside the Nile to share food and celebrate the start of the harvest season, eating foods such as lettuce, considered symbolic of fertility and renewal. The Jewish Passover is also celebrated on the first Full Moon following the first New Moon after the Spring Equinox. The Christian festival of Easter, which is also lunar, often falls in March. Witches and Wiccans usually use the name Ostara for this festival, although Druids may know it as Alban Eilir.

> *'To him is the winged secret flame and to her the stooping starlight.'*
>
> —Poem from *The Book of the Law*, Aleister Crowley, 1904

20 MARCH

FEAST OF THE SUPREME RITUAL

This rite marks Aleister Crowley's Invocation to Horus in 1904 (see page 188). It is observed by those who follow Thelema, the spiritual philosophy created by Crowley, which focuses on Egyptian gods. In five parts, it ends with a renunciation of the old Aeon, or age, and the 'slave gods'. Occultist Crowley believed that it initiated a new era for humanity. On the following day (or separately on the same day), the Equinox of the Gods marks the start of the Thelemic New Year. This celebrates the shift of the Aeon, the astrological era, from the Age of Osiris to the Age of Horus.

RITUALS, SPELLS & DIVINATION

RITUALS & SPELLWORK

March rituals tend to focus on the Spring Equinox and the renewal of life. You may want to rise at dawn, to watch the sunrise, and remain awake until sunset, observing the balance of this particular time of year.

Spring Equinox rituals in particular celebrate balance and the gradual return of the light. They may also include a celebration of fertility. If creating a spring altar, be sure to include plenty of new greenery and possibly a basket of eggs (a symbol of fertility).

You can carry out fire rituals, with a nod to Aries and its fiery energy, or work with the Kabbalistic sphere of Gevurah (strength and vigour). Burn red candles to gain courage and confidence and place stones such as red jasper on an altar, if you have one. You can also add sacred weaponry (handled carefully and safely) such as a sword, to help envisage the dynamic energy of this sign entering your life. Pathworking through the Kabbalistic Tree of Life can be undertaken, again, to connect with strength and courage (see page 186).

Aries also sees in new beginnings, so this can be a good time to start magical work: to remove blocks, on a piece of paper, draw an image of whatever is blocking you (you can do a two-card Tarot reading if unsure: draw a card symbolizing yourself, and then a second card to represent the block). Safely set alight your drawing in a fire-proof container, imagining the block being consumed by the energy of the flames and dissipating into ash.

INTENTION SETTING

Although leaving offerings at sacred sites is discouraged, you may want to plant some seeds in a pot in your garden at home. Set your spring intentions into a handful of quick-growing seeds, such as parsley, and plant them: as the seeds grow, so too will your intentions develop.

NUMEROLOGY

Via Jupiter, the older ruler of Pisces, March is associated numerologically with 3, representing sincerity and spiritual understanding.

Flora, the Roman goddess of flowers and spring, in *The Goddess Flora* by Luca Giordano, *c.*1697.

CELESTIAL MAGIC

Pagans often associate the Spring Equinox with a wild, uncertain energy as the tides of the year shift. It is an expansive time, when the light begins to grow, and we can connect with this energy to look outwards.

MOONS

The March Full Moon is sometimes known as the Worm Moon, a name granted to it by southern Native American peoples due to the earthworm casts that appear when the land begins to warm and thaw. Indigenous peoples further north refer to it as the Blue Sap Moon, when maple sap begins to rise. Magical connections with this moon involve growth and development.

METEOR SKIES

Showers include the xi Herculids, the eta Ophiuchids (mid-March) and the delta Pavonids towards month's end.

The Spring Equinox, or Ostara (around 21 March) sees day and night at nearly equal length. For many, it signifies the beginning of spring, and renewal and growth.

ELEMENTAL & ZODIAC CORRESPONDENCES

March sees Pisces move into Aries, the sign of the Ram and the start of the zodiac. Water also shifts to Fire, signalling a more dynamic and outgoing period. Aries, a sign of heat, passion and drive, propels the zodiac forwards.

Water

Neptune

PLANETARY CORRESPONDENCES

March corresponds to Neptune and then to Mars, a vital force of war, action and passion. Occultists may work with Mars in the form of the Kabbalistic sphere of Gevurah (justice and divine strength).

Fire

Mars

TAROT CORRESPONDENCES

Fire is the element of the suit of Wands, and the sphere of Gevurah is related to the Fives, which have aspects of severity and aggression. Aries corresponds to The Emperor, often shown seated on a throne bearing representations of the Ram.

SYMBOLS

March symbols include Neptune, ♆, ruler of Pisces, ♓, and Aries, ♈, ruled by Mars, ♂, the astrological symbol representing the shield and spear of the god (also the symbol of the male sex). In alchemy, the symbol for Mars is associated with iron (see also 'Bloodstone', page 57).

EARTHLY CONNECTIONS

Plants & Trees

VIOLET (*VIOLA*)

Esoteric Associations: protection, dreaming.

Uses: Traditionally seen as a protection against evil. Romans threw violets on to ancestral graves during *Dies violantionis* (Day of Mourning) on 22 March. The flowers can be dried and used in an incense or placed in a pillow to promote magical dreams.

NETTLE (*URTICA DIOICA*)

Esoteric Associations: healing, purification.

Uses: Nettle forms part of the Saxon 'nine herbs charm' for healing. Throughout the Celtic lands, nettles were thought to grow from the bodies of the dead – probably as they grow on graves – which was seen as an otherworldly element helpful in purification rituals and funerary magic. It can also be used as part of an incense in fire rituals, or in rituals to Mars himself.

CLEAVERS (*GALIUM APERINE*)

Esoteric Associations: binding, cleansing, protection.

Uses: Known for its 'sticky' nature, cleavers is thought to bind a negative energy to its source. It can also be used as a cleansing herb for the body, in the form of a spring tonic. Use in Spring Equinox rituals for its protective element, or make skeins of cleavers to help bind protective magic to oneself.

BURDOCK (*ARCTIUM LAPPA*)

Esoteric Associations: healing, empowerment, protection.

Uses: Burdock burrs stick to fur or human clothes, and are said to be useful in binding magic and to enhance creativity. If you harvest the roots in spring, the plant can then be used in a floorwash, or a small quantity of the root can be used in incense to banish negative energies.

Gemstones

AQUAMARINE

Esoteric Associations: strength, clarity, peace of mind, communication.

Uses: Considered to be a stone of spiritual growth, aquamarine was carried as a talisman by sailors. It is also connected to the Throat Chakra and is said to enhance communication.

BLOODSTONE

Esoteric Associations: strength, grounding, stability, protection.

Uses: This dark-green chalcedony is streaked with red. It stabilizes and protects against negative energies. Rich in iron, it also lends energy and vitality.

Runes

TIWAZ ✦ 27 FEBRUARY–14 MARCH

T: Tyr, the sky god. This rune denotes leadership and justice and can be invoked to give aid in legal matters.

BERKANO ✦ 14–30 MARCH

B: Berchta, the birch-goddess. Berkano represents new beginnings and fresh starts.

The hare of the Moon

FOLKLORE & MYTH

HARE LORE

In European folklore, witches can transform themselves into hares: the story of the man who throws a stone at a hare to scare it away from the crops, to then find that his elderly neighbour is suffering from a leg injury, is found all across Europe. Hares are also held to be witches' familiars and 'mad March hares' are linked to this month. Outside Europe, the hare is a prominent image in Chinese astrology, being the fourth animal of the Chinese zodiac and associated with immortality: the hare of the Moon prepares herbs in a mortar to confer immortality (see Chang'e, page 148).

MARTENITSA

In Bulgaria, Grandmother March's moods are said to affect the weather, but she can be appeased by the Martenitsa, when people wear talismans (often bracelets) that can take the form of two little people – Pizho (white, male, for purity) and Penda (red, female, for vitality). When you spot the first signs of spring, such as a stork or a flowering tree, you can remove the talisman and tie it to a tree.

DROWNING OF MARZANNA

This Polish custom, held 21 March, is a 'farewell to winter', in which a straw figure is thrown into the local river, sometimes set on fire first, to symbolize the end of winter. Today, people usually take their Marzanna dolly for a walk instead.

CHICHÉN ITZÁ

At this pre-Columbian archaeological site in Yucatán, people gather to watch an optical illusion during the Spring Equinox, in which the patterns of light and shadow reveal the feathered serpent god, Kukulcán, 'sliding' down the side of the Kukulcán pyramid. At the ancient Mesoamerican site Teotihuacán, near Mexico City, many people also dress in white and gather to observe the Equinox.

SPRING EGGS

In China, children balance eggs on a flat surface during the Spring Equinox – if your egg stands up, it's a sign of good luck. This is attributed to the alignment of the Earth at the time of the Equinox, but it's actually a result of the yolk sinking down and stabilizing the egg.

IV

APRIL

April's leaves unfurl and crops are underway. The occult tide of springtime is in full flood, and we can build on March's magical work. April is associated with Venus, beginning with the Ancient Roman festival of the Veneralia on the first and ending with the great European witches' sabbat of Walpurgis Night on 30 April.

THEMES & ENTITIES

The name April comes from Latin and may derive from the Greek Aphrillis, an appellation of Aphrodite, or from the verb *aperire*, to open. The Saxons called this month *ēastre-monaþ*, which may be why we term the great Christian festival of this month Easter.

APHRODITE (VENUS)

Early worship of Aphrodite may derive from the cult of the Mesopotamian goddess Ishtar: in parts of the ancient world, she was a goddess of war, though she is a goddess of love and desire. As Venus, on 1 April she was honoured with myrtle garlands in the Roman Veneralia festival. Her symbols are doves, seashells, roses and myrtle.

FREYA

This Norse goddess of love is the northern equivalent to Venus and daughter of the sea god Njord. She is a member of the Vanir, Norse gods associated with fertility and wisdom. Freya also welcomes half of the souls of all slain warriors into her hall, Sessrúmnir. She rides on a chariot drawn by cats, or sometimes rides on a wild boar.

ARCHANGEL ARIEL

ANGELIC CORRESPONDENCE

Known as the 'lion of God' in Hebrew, Ariel is an angel of nature, and a healer of animals and plants. Ariel was depicted as a lion-headed entity, and is described by occultist Cornelius Agrippa as a demon as well as an angel.

ASMODEL

ANGELIC CORRESPONDENCE

Asmodel is linked to both April and the zodiac sign of Taurus. He is an angel of rebirth and patience.

BELPHEGOR

DEMONIC CORRESPONDENCE

This Lord of the Gap is associated with the seven deadly sins in the Christian tradition. Identified as the demon of sloth, he may derive from a Levantine deity, Baal Peor.

SABBATS, FESTIVALS & CELEBRATIONS

April's festivals centre on the celebration of spring, continuing on from those held at the Spring Equinox, and acknowledging the growing fertility of the land. The principal pagan celebration in April is Walpurgis Night, held at the end of the month. It is a significant date for witches in particular, as the year turns towards the great festival of Beltane in May.

30 APRIL TO 1 MAY

○ *WALPURGIS NIGHT*

✳ On Walpurgisnacht, 30 April, or May Eve, through to 1 May, witches are said to gather on the mountain plateau of the Hexentanzplatz (thought to be the site of a Saxon sacrificial ground) in Germany, in order to dance and meet the Devil before flying to the mountain of the Brocken.

The name itself refers to the eighth-century Abbess Walpurga, now Saint Walpurga, as Walpurgisnacht occurs on the eve of her saint's day – ironically, she was known for fighting witchcraft.

Walpurgis Night is known to be a supernatural time, with elements of transgression, rebellion and freedom. It is a transitional period, when bonfires are lit to remove the last traces of winter and to welcome in the summer's energy.

A thirteenth-century poem depicts the Brocken summit (the Brockengipfel) as a place where ghosts meet. In Germany it is called Tanz in den Mai, or Dancing into May, when dances might be held. You may also leave Ankenschnitt

KEY ○ Historical Event ✳ Annual Event ◇ Variable Dates

(buttered bread with honey) on the doorstep for spectral hounds accompanying their master, the Devil, out on this important night.

Modern witches and pagans often observe this night, and so do modern Satanists: the Church of Satan was established on Walpurgis Night in 1966, in San Francisco. Founder Anton LaVey noted in *The Satanic Bible* that Walpurgis Night, Hallowe'en and one's birthday are the most important dates in the Satanist calendar.

SEPTEMBER TO APRIL

ODO FESTIVAL

The biannual Odo Festival in Nigeria is celebrated by the Ngwo people of Enugu – the word derives from *odomagana* (masquerade) and relates to the period when the ancestral dead return to visit the living. Participants wear lavish, complex masks and engage in a series of sacred dances and rituals. This festival sometimes culminates in April, but note that it is held according to ancestral cycles and does not have fixed dates.

'Now to the Brocken the witches ride;
The stubble is gold and the corn is green;
There is the carnival crew to be seen,
And Squire Urianus will come to preside.
So over the valleys our company floats,
With witches a-farting on stinking old goats.'

—*Faust*, Johann Wolfgang von Goethe

RITUALS, SPELLS & DIVINATION

INTENTION & VISUALIZATION

The eve of Beltane at the end of April is a powerful time for visualization. If you are undertaking intention work, perhaps write your intention, then visualize how it might best be made manifest. You could undertake a Kabbalistic pathworking – a visualization beginning in the sphere of Chokmah (wisdom), associated with Neptune. Imagine the creative spark of Aries emerging from a vast ocean, and coming to rest on the palm of your hand. This spark can be changed into an aim (such as a new job). Imagine yourself moving along the pathway between Chokmah and Chesed (mercy), the sphere of Jupiter, a path ruled by Taurus: walk away from the great sea, towards your completed goal within Chesed (see also page 186).

HEXENNACHT

Satanists hold rituals on Walpurgis Night, which is mentioned in the Satanic Bible as 'the fruition of the Spring Equinox', but some sects may commemorate the slightly different festival of Hexennacht, in which they honour those who have been victimized by superstition. This may take the form of a memorial ritual or private meditation, and rituals that emphasize the importance of knowledge and critical thinking might also feature.

THE BOOK OF THE LAW

Thelemites follow the reading of *The Book of the Law, Liber AL vel Legis*, said to have been channelled to Aleister Crowley (see page 188) in 1904 by the Egyptian deities Nuit, Hadit and Ra-Hoor-Khuit. The ritual begins at noon on 8 April and ends at noon on 10 April. Sections of *The Book of the Law* are read along with other Thelemic rituals such as the Gnostic Mass (Liber XV), which are not specific to this month. Regular rituals within Thelemic practice might also be carried out.

NUMEROLOGY

April's number is 9, relating to Mars, the ruler of Aries. As befits Mars, 9 represents courage, passion and independence.

An Incantation Scene by Frans Francken the Younger, 1606.

CELESTIAL MAGIC

April's night skies are marked by the Spring Triangle of Arcturus, Spica and Regulus, while its astrological energies relate to Fire and Earth. Mars and Venus are the dominant planets of April.

MOONS

April's Full Moon is known as the Pink Moon by some Native American peoples, after the phlox wildflower that blooms at this time. It's also known as Egg Moon for when the birds start nesting, Sprouting Grass Moon and Breaking Ice Moon, likely because this is when ice begins to melt in some regions.

METEOR SKIES

The Lyrids, a meteor shower that is the debris from a comet, appear mid-month (16–25 April). The Eta Aquariids also appear throughout April to May.

Pink Moon, so-called due to the illuminated pink phlox blossom at this time of year.

ELEMENTAL & ZODIAC CORRESPONDENCES

April starts with Fire (Aries) and moves into Earth (Taurus). Its initial fiery Aries energy becomes muted by Taurus, which roots and grounds this spark, allowing us to make it manifest in the earthly realm. Taurus is one of the oldest constellations, the Bull of Heaven that the goddess Ishtar sends to fight the hero Gilgamesh.

PLANETARY CORRESPONDENCES

April's planets are Mars, representing Aries, and Venus, which corresponds with Taurus. In the Kabbalistic Tree of Life, Mars is linked with the sephirah of Gevurah (the sphere of masculinity, structure and boundary) and Venus with Netzach (the sphere of femininity and female sovereignty), in a balance.

TAROT CORRESPONDENCES

Taurus is associated with the Tarot card of The Hierophant, which represents spiritual authority. Aries is linked to The Emperor, which can be a card of restriction and rigidity.

SYMBOLS

This month's astrological symbols are Mars, ♂ (representing Aries, ♈), and Venus, ♀ (representing Taurus, ♉).

EARTHLY CONNECTIONS

Plants & Trees

MUGWORT (*ARTEMISIA VULGARIS*)

Esoteric Associations: visualization, divination.

Uses: A 'witches' herb' with links to the Moon (*artemisia* comes from Artemis, the Roman huntress and moon goddess with correlations to Diana) and to St John's Eve, when it can traditionally be picked (see page 98). It is often used in divinatory magic, as a wash to cleanse scrying balls or mirrors and to heighten psychic abilities. Place it under pillows to promote prophetic dreams.

MINT (*MENTHA*)

Esoteric Associations: cleansing, clearing, concentration.

Uses: In Ancient Greece mint was consumed in a sacred drink during the secret rites known as the Eleusinian Mysteries, and peppermint has been found in Egyptian tombs. Pliny recommends wearing a crown of mint to 'aid mental processes'. It is said to sharpen concentration and cleanse the mind – its oil can be used in ritual baths.

ROSE (*ROSA*)

Esoteric Associations: love, Venus, royal houses.

Uses: For love spells – use rose in incense, potpourri or charms (hang in a small bag around your neck) to attract love to oneself, or in a massage oil with sandalwood (see page 28) as an aphrodisiac.

ALDER (*ALNUS*)

Esoteric Associations: death, protection.

Uses: This fourth tree in the Celtic tree calendar (18 March–14 April, see page 187) can produce a red pigment used in dyes. If you are working magically with alder, use it to invoke a protective, warrior energy (see page 72).

Gemstones

DIAMOND

Esoteric Associations: strength, purity, clarity, truth.

Uses: Diamond (from the Greek, *adamas*, meaning 'invincible') is said to grow dull in the presence of a liar.

CLEAR QUARTZ

Esoteric Associations: clarity, divination.

Uses: Clear crystal balls are often made of quartz and thus there is an association with seeing into the future. It is said to amplify energy.

Runes

EHWAZ ✦ 30 MARCH–14 APRIL

E: Horse, two horses. A sign of travel and journeys, but also of one's efforts coming to fruition.

MANNAZ ✦ 14–29 APRIL

M: Man, mankind. Relates to the inner self but also to community and responsibility towards others.

FOLKLORE & MYTH

APRIL FOOL'S DAY

This may be connected to the Ancient Roman festival of the Hilaria, celebrated towards the end of March, which featured pranks and mischievous tricks. Some historians claim that April Fool's originated in France in the 1580s, when the calendar was changed and the date of the New Year switched from 1 April to 1 January, and people who failed to realize this were sent out on 'fool's errands'. In the UK, the 'day' lasts until noon, beyond which time tricks can no longer be played.

WATER POURING

These festivals and ceremonies, often astrologically inspired, are conducted across Asia, often in April, and can include boisterously throwing water at one another as well as pouring scented water over the hands of older relatives to show respect. The festival of Songkran in Thailand marks the passage from Pisces to Aries and the start of the solar new year. Thingyan in Myanmar also marks the start of the new year by throwing water, in a symbolic 'washing away' of the sins and bad luck of the previous year.

QINGMING FESTIVAL

In China and some other Asian cultures, Qingming Festival in early April involves sweeping the tombs of ancestors as well as burning joss and making offerings such as traditional food to them. The origins of this festival are very old, dating back over two thousand years.

KHA B-NISAN

This means 'First of April' in Aramaic (Syriac) and is celebrated as a New Year's celebration in parts of Turkey, Syria, Iran and Iraq among the Assyrian community. Its origins lie in the Babylonian Akitu festival, which dates back thousands of years. Nowadays, traditional clothes are worn and participants dance, cook special food and recite poetry.

ALDER LEGENDS

In the folklore of Ireland and Northern Europe, the alder (see page 71) has a dark reputation and is closely associated with death – in Danish legend, the Alder King steals children away. When the wood is cut, it quickly turns from white to blood red, and thus the tree is also associated with blood and war.

'If every fool wore a crown, we should all be kings.'

—Welsh proverb

V

MAY

May is the month of the great pagan celebration of Beltane, once a numinous and supernatural time when the veil between our world and the spirit realm was believed to be thin and the dead might return to visit the living. Nowadays it is a festival celebrating love and sex. This is a time of fertility rites, when the rising sap of spring rushes headlong into a celebration of love itself.

THEMES & ENTITIES

May takes its name from the Latin *Maius*. It is a time of year when flowers are reaching their peak and many of this month's correspondences, such as the names of the moons, reflect this.

MAIA

May is connected to the Greek mountain nymph Maia (one of the seven sisters in Greek myth known as the Pleiades) and to Maia Majesta, a Roman goddess of spring. Linked to fertility, she is mother of the god Hermes – in Ancient Rome, a pregnant sow was said to be sacrificed to her on 1 May. Maia and her sisters are also companions to Artemis, goddess of the Moon and of hunting.

CERNUNNOS/HORNED GOD/PAN

Sometimes confused with the Christian devil, this god is not connected to Satan. The image of the Horned God, also known as Cernunnos, and connected at times with the mischievous god Pan, appears in cave art and on the Iron Age Gundestrup cauldron. He is also said to be one of the leaders of the Wild Hunt (see page 22).

AMBRIEL

ANGELIC CORRESPONDENCE

Linked with Gemini and May, Ambriel is an angel of communication, associated in modern times with technology. Aleister Crowley and the Golden Dawn (see page 188) linked him with the Queen of Cups, a Tarot card of introspection, and he is regarded by the Catholic Church as an angel of protection.

MARBAS

DEMONIC CORRESPONDENCE

Sometimes linked with this month, Marbas can be depicted as a lion-headed figure, and is known for both causing and curing diseases, and for assisting humans to change shape.

VALEFAR

DEMONIC CORRESPONDENCE

This demon is also connected to May by some authorities. He appears as a lion with a human head and is a Duke of Hell. He aids thieves and tempts people to steal.

SABBATS, FESTIVALS & CELEBRATIONS

For many who celebrate Beltane, May represents the start of summer: a time of fertility and abundance. May Day, the Jack in the Green and hobby 'osses' abound, alongside ancient floral festivities and rites.

28 APRIL TO EARLY MAY

○ ***FLORALIA***

✳ ◇ Though no longer practised, this Ancient Roman festival honouring the fertility, vegetation and flower goddess Flora, may have made its way into May customs today, particularly for the Jack in the Green (see page 86). Flora had her own high priest, the *flamen Florialis*. The satirist Juvenal notes that prostitutes took part in the festival, which was primarily a plebeian event (one for the general population of Rome), and Ovid tells us that hares and goats were released into the crowds as symbols of fertility. Beans and lupins were thrown at the crowds as well, and multi-coloured clothing was worn.

1 MAY

○ ***BELTANE***

✳ This old word for May has been adopted in Revivalist Paganism as the main fertility celebration on 1 May. It is celebrated by dancing around a maypole and lighting bonfires. Beltane is mentioned in the Irish *Sanas Chormaic* (Cormac's Glossary), showing its ancient roots. In Ireland on 1 May, cattle were herded between two fires for protection before they were taken up to their summer pastures. Women jumped the fire in the hope that they would meet a husband; wives did so to bring fertility.

Today, modern pagans celebrate Beltane with rituals, and many include the old elements

KEY ○ Historical Event ✳ Annual Event ◇ Variable Dates

> *'Use life's flower, while it still blooms; for the thorn . . . is flouted when the roses have fallen away.'*
>
> —Floralia excerpt from Ovid's *Fasti*

of a maypole and bonfire. There are also a number of Jack in the Green celebrations at this time of year in England, when people dress up and parade through town, surrounding the 'Jack', an ancient symbol of the wild (see page 86).

Primroses were scattered over the door in Ireland and any hares found amongst the cattle were killed, in case they were witches in disguise. In Scotland, rowan crosses were put over doors to protect inhabitants, and rowan branches were used widely at this time to protect against negative magic (see page 42).

8 MAY

WHITE LOTUS DAY

This is observed by followers of Theosophy (a spiritual movement founded in the nineteenth century, which draws on Hinduism and Buddhism) to mark the anniversary of the death of their founder, Madame Helena Blavatsky, in 1891. Blavatsky asked that her friends should meet on this day and read from Sir Edwin Arnold's book *The Light of Asia* and the Hindu scripture of the *Bhagavad Gita*. The lotus is described by Blavatsky as 'the child of the Universe bearing the likeness of its mother in its bosom': its leaves are held in miniature within its seed, symbolizing the life and development of humankind.

'Guardian of this house,
watch over it in the year
to come, till again the Bel-fire
is extinguished and relit.
Bless this house and be
blessed by it; let all who
live here, and all friends
who are welcomed here,
prosper under its roof.
So mote it be!'

—Beltane rites declaration written by
Stewart Farrar in *Eight Sabbats for Witches*

RITUALS, SPELLS & DIVINATION

BELTANE RITES & RITUALS

A traditional way to celebrate Beltane is around a maypole, with a roaring fire nearby, over which you then leap, hand in hand with a partner. Or you can simply light a candle for a time, blow it out and keep it for next Beltane.

Pagan rituals for Beltane often focus on fertility rites. These may include the declaration by Stewart Farrar (see left). You may also want to undertake a Rite to Venus (see page 62). Light pink candles and offer the goddess a bowl of roses (see page 70) floating in water, or celebrate the Horned God (see page 76) with a ritual in his honour in woodland.

DIVINATION & VISUALIZATION

Writer Jacqueline Memory Paterson suggests that in the spring, one should undertake visionary practice or spellwork reflecting 'light and life' (e.g. healing).

Magical work with May's Full Moon may involve visualizations around growth and expansion of magical projects, such as those begun at the Spring Equinox.

FERTILITY SPELL

To make a fertility charm, sew a small image of yourself and a child, decorate it with flowers, crystals and rose oil and place it on your altar. Light a red candle for fertility and call upon one of the deities associated with Beltane for aid.

NUMEROLOGY

May's number is 6, relating to Venus and thus representing love, beauty and fertility.

CELESTIAL MAGIC

The clearer, gentler weather of May often offers good opportunities for observing the Moon and the summer constellations of Leo and Virgo, which are more prominent at this time of year.

MOONS

May's Full Moon is often called the Flower Moon. The Cherokee, Dakota and Lakota peoples of North America also call it the Planting Moon. These names signify a time of floral growth and indicate the essential time of year to plant seeds for crops.

METEOR SKIES

The Eta Aquariid meteor shower – debris from Halley's Comet – appears each May in the Northern and Southern Hemispheres.

The Great Comet of 1456 (Halley's Comet)

Earth Venus

Air Mercury

ELEMENTAL & ZODIAC CORRESPONDENCES

May is associated with Earth, for Taurus, and then Air, for Gemini, also known as the Twins, who are a reference to the Graeco-Roman myth of Castor and Pollux. They are the sons of Leda, a Spartan queen; they have different fathers, and in some legends they are the brothers of Helen of Troy. When the mortal Castor dies, his twin Pollux asks his father Zeus if the brothers can be joined immortally. Zeus places them in the heavens as the Gemini constellation. Patrons of travellers, they are said to appear in the form of St Elmo's fire to aid seafarers. They are also patrons of athletes and have equestrian links, possibly to Indo-European horse deities. The Twins were worshipped in Sparta, where the pear tree was considered sacred to them.

PLANETARY CORRESPONDENCES

Planetary associations for May are Venus and Mercury. Venus is connected to the sphere of Netzach, while Mercury is linked to Hod.

TAROT CORRESPONDENCES

The Tarot trump of The Lovers is linked to Gemini, but the sign is also sometimes connected to The Magician, a card of cunning and knowledge.

SYMBOLS

May's astrological symbols are Gemini, ♊, Venus, ♀, then Taurus, ♉, and Mercury, ☿.

EARTHLY CONNECTIONS

Plants & Trees

WILLOW (*SALIX*)

Esoteric Associations: Moon, unconscious, feminine, water, music, luck, protection, Hecate, Orpheus.

Uses: Willow (*saille* in Irish) is the fifth tree of the Celtic tree calendar (15 April–12 May, see page 187) and is used in some funeral customs. Mourning garlands were woven from willow stems, or withies (although in Scandinavia it was considered unlucky for willow to be present at a funeral). In Irish folklore, it is sometimes linked to cheerfulness and good fortune: tying strips of willow around a milk churn is thought to produce a good yield of milk, while carrying willow twigs with you on a journey is meant to protect you against harm.

CLOVER (*TRIFOLIUM*)

Esoteric Association: luck (to find a four-leafed one).

Uses: Can be used as an ingredient in banishing magic. It also has a connection with the Tarot via the modern playing card deck, with the three-lobed image of the clubs becoming the suit of Wands in the Minor Arcana of the Tarot deck.

WOODRUFF (*GALIUM ODORATUM*)

Esoteric Associations: beginning of summer, Beltane, vitality, protection, prosperity.

Uses: Woodruff is an ingredient in Beltane wine. Its planet is Mars and its element is fire. Carrying it is said to attract money and prosperity, offer protection against negative magic and guard against curses.

Gemstone

EMERALD

Esoteric Associations: growth, renewal.

Uses: May's birthstone is said to be able to break spells and to cure the sick. Placed under the tongue, emerald in legend is said to help someone to predict the future. Some believe this gem can also be used to invoke demons.

Runes

LAGUZ ✦ 29 APRIL–14 MAY

L: Water, or a leek. Relates to cleansing, intuition and to the opening up of creativity and psychic powers.

INGWAZ ✦ 14–29 MAY

NG: Ing, the earth god. Relates to the need to re-establish our connections with the natural world.

FOLKLORE & MYTH

JACK IN THE GREEN

This English May Day celebration involves 'Jack', a person – or a large effigy – dressed in leaves to represent a form of nature spirit. The Jack parades through town, followed by his retinue, who also dress up. The day often ends with the 'slaying' of the Jack, in a ritual battle. He is symbolically hit with sticks, and his leaves are torn off, to release the spirit of summer (see 'Beltane', page 78).

'Jack in the Green,
Jack in the Green,
and we'll all dance
each springtime with
Jack in the Green . . .'

—May Day festival chorus

WELL DRESSING

In some Gloucestershire and Derbyshire villages, there is a procession and the local well or spring is decorated with elaborate patterns of flowers along with mosaics made of seeds, petals and leaves on a bed of clay. The custom is said to celebrate the fresh water given by the springs and wells, but may date from a time when the spirits of these places were venerated.

WILLOW & MYTH

The Greek hero Orpheus is reputed to have carried willow with him as protection on his journey to the Underworld – the tree was thought to be sacred to the goddesses there, particularly Hecate (see page 146), who was believed to use willow for her wands. In Ireland, harps were made from its wood.

THE BENDIDIA

Some Hellenic reconstructionists and pagans celebrate the Ancient Greek Bendidia around 28 May as a family feast day or in rites to Bendis, the Thracian goddess of the Moon (the Dark Moon, particularly) and of the Underworld.

Jack in the Green

VI

JUNE

June is the month of the Summer Solstice, falling on or around 21 June. It is the longest day of the year, before the nights begin to lengthen, and when 'the virtues of herbs are strongest', so it's a good time to gather them. In June, Stonehenge and other sacred sites often feature a ritually enacted battle between winter and summer.

THEMES & ENTITIES

June comes from the Latin *Iunius*, 'sacred to Juno'. The goddess's own name may come from the Latin for 'young', denoting a vital, fertile energy.

JUNO (HERA)

As a goddess of marriage and fertility, Juno was revered throughout the ancient world and she is worshipped by some modern pagans today. Her sacred bird is the peacock. Juno is the mother of a number of gods, including Mars and Vulcan, but she also has a warrior aspect and is often depicted in armour and carrying a shield – she is protector, wife and mother. Scholars link her to the Moon: although she is not a moon goddess, some of her ancient epithets relate to the waxing and waning of the Moon's phases.

ÁINE

This Irish fertility goddess is said to have died of grief on St John's Eve, after her daughters married against her wishes– she was honoured by torches carried through the fields. She is also claimed to be a lake-dwelling entity who emerges on Midsummer Eve, and in County Limerick she was acknowledged as Queen of the Fae.

MURIEL

ANGELIC CORRESPONDENCE

Governing power of intuition and empathy, Muriel is linked to the zodiac sign of Cancer and is a peace bringer, often invoked to resolve conflicts. However, in some apocryphal texts, she is linked to the angel of Death, Abaddon.

VINE

DEMONIC CORRESPONDENCE

Scholar Johann Wier says of Vine that the demon, who is a king and an earl, '... showeth himselfe as a lion, riding on a blacke horsse, and carrieth a viper in his hand, he gladlie buildeth large towres, he throweth downe stone walles, and maketh waters rough.'

PAIMON

DEMONIC CORRESPONDENCE

Paimon manifests as a man with a female face, riding on a dromedary. He is said to have been one of the cherubim before the Fall.

SABBATS, FESTIVALS & CELEBRATIONS

Both the Summer Solstice (Litha) and Midsummer celebrate June's long days of sunlight as well as the transition to the gradual 'drawing in' that points us to the Winter Solstice.

20 OR 21 JUNE

○ ✳ ◇ ***SUMMER SOLSTICE / LITHA OR ALBAN HERUIN/ALBAN HEFIN (DRUIDIC)***

The word 'solstice' comes from the Latin words for 'sun' and 'to stand still', so it is sometimes known as the 'sunstanding'.

As one of the four main quarter days, Litha is considered to be one of the most significant festivals in the Wheel of the Year and is celebrated ritually by most people who follow a pagan path. It is also held by some forms of modern paganism to be the point at which the Holly King (winter) 'triumphs' over the Oak King (summer).

The Summer Solstice is celebrated as a spiritual event by Wiccans and Druids, and as a folklore celebration globally. In parts of Europe (it is a national holiday in Sweden and Finland) it has older roots: it is a fire festival, celebrated with bonfires and dancing. In Britain, people gather at dawn at Stonehenge to celebrate the return of the Sun. A number of stone circles, such as Stonehenge, Calanais (Isle of Lewis, Scotland) and the Rollrights (England), are believed by scholars to align with the Summer Solstice. Ales Stenar in Sweden and Carnac in Brittany also seem to have been built in alignment with this solar event.

KEY ○ Historical Event ✳ Annual Event ◇ Variable Dates

24 JUNE

INTI RAYMI

This Inca festival is held to celebrate the Southern Hemisphere's Winter Solstice and the sun god Inti. It was originally celebrated with animal sacrifice to the Earth mother goddess Pachamama, and celebrations of food and drink, such as corn cakes prepared by the 'chosen women' (known as Virgins of the Sun), took place after a period of abstinence. Revived in the 1940s, the ceremony takes place again today at the archaeological site of Sacsayhuaman, although the sacrifices are now symbolic.

24 JUNE

MIDSUMMER (ST JOHN THE BAPTIST DAY)

In one of Shakespeare's most famous plays – *A Midsummer Night's Dream* – magic and mayhem rule at Midsummer, when the fairy folk wreak havoc on mortals. Some modern pagans prefer to undertake rituals around this time rather than celebrate the Summer Solstice. Midsummer is also the feast day of the Roman goddess Fortuna, when a procession was held along the river Tiber to her temple. In modern times, midsummer tends to be celebrated on the Saturday nearest to 24 June.

'Sun at peak, so bold and bright,
Longest day and shortest night.
Fire above, and earth below,
Bless the seeds we've come to grow.'

—Pagan Summer Solstice chant

RITUALS, SPELLS & DIVINATION

PAGAN RITUALS

Once, people lit bonfires on St John's Eve (Midsummer Eve) to celebrate the rising Sun, and rolled burning wheels down hills – perhaps to symbolize the Sun in its path. Today, we may celebrate the Summer Solstice by staying up all night and seeing in the dawn, or might prefer to recognize Midsummer (24 June).

Pagans may invoke any of the solar deities at this time of year – Ra, Ceridwen in her aspect as the goddess of the coming harvest (see page 104), Sekhmet, or Bast (a solar deity before she became a lunar one), Sol or Sunna (both female, and both of Germanic origin), Apollo (see page 104), Helios or the Aztec god Huitzilopochtli.

In the central part of the ritual, pagans may welcome in the Sun by reciting a poem or a prayer, or by re-enacting the battle between the Holly and Oak Kings (see page 92).

TAROT DIVINATION

In Tarot, the Justice card is strongly associated with June. It is also one of the powerful female archetypes of the Major Arcana and represents balance and fairness. If you draw this card during this month, it suggests that a lot of uncertainty will become resolved and you should be in a much more secure position once you've come through the decision-making process.

OIL OF HYPERICUM

Steep a handful of St John's Wort petals (see page 98) in a small jar of sunflower oil for a few weeks, until the oil becomes thoroughly infused. You can then use it to anoint a golden or orange candle and ask the herb for its protection.

NUMEROLOGY

One of June's zodiac signs is Gemini – its ruler, Mercury, is associated with the number 5, and with knowledge, intelligence and understanding.

'Power of the Sun,
we honour you this night.
We leap across the
fire to keep our
spirits bright.'

—Pagan/Wiccan chant honouring the Sun

CELESTIAL MAGIC

June's bright night sky includes the Summer Triangle of Vega, Deneb and Altair. Air moves to Water as we turn from Gemini to Cancer.

STRAWBERRY MOON

June's Full Moon gets its name from Indigenous peoples in North America noting that it was the time of the harvest season for wild strawberries.

METEOR SKIES

The Boötid meteor shower appears in the Northern Hemisphere in late June.

ELEMENTAL & ZODIAC CORRESPONDENCES

June begins in Air (Gemini) and shifts to Water as the zodiac moves into the sign of Cancer. Its name comes from the monstrous crab Karkinos, which the goddess Hera placed in the sky after Hercules crushed it. In Ancient Egypt, Cancer was represented by a scarab beetle

The Northern Hemisphere view of the faintest constellation – Cancer. It is located between Leo and Gemini and is visible from December to June.

– the Mesopotamians used the image of a turtle. Both creatures were held to push the Sun across the sky, starting the Summer Solstice. The month also has a strong connection with the Fire element.

Air

Mercury

PLANETARY CORRESPONDENCES

The Moon, Cancer's governing planet, is linked to the Kabbalistic sephirah of Yesod, a sphere of psychic gifts that contains the spark of inspiration and is linked to the unconscious and intuition. Mercury, ruler of Gemini, is connected to the sephirah of Hod, the sphere of the mind and of communication.

Water

Moon

TAROT CORRESPONDENCES

The Lovers card connects to Gemini, while Cancer is linked to The Chariot, a card of opposing forces brought into balance. Cancer also corresponds to The Moon card, often featuring a crayfish or lobster emerging from the waters of the unconscious. The card most commonly associated with June is Justice, representing balance and fairness (see page 94).

SYMBOLS

June's astrological symbols are Mercury, ☿, relating to Gemini, ♊, and the Moon, ☽, relating to Cancer, ♋.

EARTHLY CONNECTIONS

Plants & Trees

ST JOHN'S WORT (*HYPERICUM PERFORATUM*)

Esoteric Associations: positivity, illumination.

Uses: The name *hypericum* comes from the words 'hyper' and 'ikon', as it was hung over pictures of St John on the saint's day in order to ward off evil. As a solar herb, its positive and light-giving qualities are said to shine into dark shadowy places and illuminate them. It treated psychiatric disorders in the Middle Ages, and was considered to ward off negative magic and demons. The herbalist Mrs Grieve gives us a different meaning of the name: 'Its name Hypericum is derived from the Greek and means "over an apparition", a reference to the belief that the herb was so obnoxious to evil spirits that a whiff of it would cause them to fly'. Note that another plant, Mugwort, is called St John's herb, and is also traditionally picked on St John's Eve (see page 70).

MEADOWSWEET (*FILIPENDULA ULMARIA*)

Esoteric Associations: change, transformation, marriage, funerals, transitions.

Uses: Meadowsweet, also known as 'Bridewort', was once used in marriage celebrations. It is sometimes held to be one of the three sacred herbs of the Druids, and its pollen is often found at ritual sites. Magically, it can be used in love charms and spells, and also in funeral rites.

HAWTHORN (*CRATAEGUS*)

Esoteric Associations: protection, bad fortune, faeries.

Uses: It is said to be unlucky to bring flowering hawthorn (may) into the house, and much Irish and Celtic folklore tells of its Otherworld connections. It was also believed to have a protective side, and was planted around farms to keep negative magic away from cattle and crops.

Gemstones

MOONSTONE

Esoteric Associations: water, Moon.

Uses: June's birthstone can enhance intuition and connect with the unconscious mind.

PEARL

Esoteric Associations: wisdom, positive outcome from difficulty.

Uses: Carry a pearl if you are going through a difficult time.

ALEXANDRITE

Esoteric Associations: Cancer, Neptune, ocean.

Uses: For vizualization in water and Moon rituals, and in Kabbalistic pathworking.

Runes

OTHALA ✦ 29 MAY–14 JUNE

O: Ancestral property. Grounds us in the place where we reside; the culmination of our efforts; a time of peace.

DAGAZ ✦ 14–29 JUNE

D: Day or dawn. Symbolizes new beginnings and the illumination that comes with the breaking dawn.

FOLKLORE & MYTH

IVAN KUPALA

An Eastern European holiday celebrated in Ukraine and Belarus, this Midsummer festival involves leaping over bonfires, bathing naked in rivers and making flower wreaths that, when placed in a river, can help foretell marriage. At midnight a magical fern flower is said to bloom in the depths of the forest, guarded by forest spirits.

HAWTHORN MAGIC

This sixth tree in the Celtic tree calendar (13 May–9 June, see page 187) is often held to be a gateway into the Otherworld. Around 103 hawthorns (may, or *huathe* in the Ogham alphabet) can be found at sacred wells in Ireland, with rags tied to their branches to honour the tree and the faery people. The hawthorn near Glastonbury's Chalice Well often bears blossom and fruit at the same time and the old may trees of Glastonbury are said to have sprung from the staff of Joseph of Arimathea as he planted it in the earth of Wearyall Hill.

The Night of Ivan Kupala
by Klavdy Lebedev (1852–1916).

MIDSUMMER DAY

In folklore, it is said that if you wish to make your vegetable garden flourish then having a naked woman walk through it at Midsummer will make it thrive.

PHI TA KHON

Celebrated in Thailand, this celebration falls between March and July (a date is selected by local mediums). Protection from the Mun river spirit is sought by participants, who wear ghost masks and perform dances.

'If Midsummer Day be ever so little rainy, the hazel and walnut will be scarce; corn smitten in many places; but apples, pears and plums will not be hurt.'

—Traditional folklore saying

VII

JULY

Sometimes called the 'hearth of summer', July is a time when this season is at its height: the harvest is coming to fruition and building up to the great pagan harvest celebration of Lughnasadh, or Lammas, on 1 August. This is a time to undertake magical work relating to abundance, courage and empowerment, even though the days are beginning to grow shorter after the Summer Solstice.

THEMES & ENTITIES

July's magical work leads up to the harvest festival of Lammas, with projects coming to fruition after the energetic drive and initial impetus of the spring. This is a time for connecting with the fiery energies of the summer, focusing on empowerment and strength.

CERRIDWEN (CERIDWEN)

Some pagans celebrate Welsh goddess Cerridwen on 3 July. She is treated as a harvest deity now, though sixteenth-century texts refer to her as an enchantress and the guardian of a magical Cauldron of Knowledge. In modern paganism she has links with The Empress Tarot card, along with the harvest deity Demeter (see page 132).

APOLLO

Apollo the sun god takes the Trojans' side in the Trojan war. Originally a possible Hittite deity, he is also an archer, a colonizer, a healer, a builder and a god of prophecy. Many things are sacred to him: the lyre, the bow, the swan, the crow, the tamarisk, the wolf, the serpent and the laurel.

NEPTUNE

This deity is the Roman equivalent of Poseidon, the god of the sea, and also a protector against drought. His origins may also lie in the Etruscan god Nethuns. Neptune's festival, the Neptunalia, was held on 23 July.

VERCHIEL

ANGELIC CORRESPONDENCE

Occultist Franz Bardon notes that Verchiel (ruler of Leo) 'controls all life in all spheres, on all planets (including our earth), whether it concerns the life in the plant, animal or human kingdoms or whether it concerns the human being in his physical, astral or mental body.'

SERATTIEL (SARATIEL)

DEMONIC CORRESPONDENCE

The demonic king of the sign of Leo, his name means 'the Cutting of God'. Some regard him as a form of spirit rather than a demon.

SABBATS, FESTIVALS & CELEBRATIONS

July is a time of ripening and fulfilment, featuring many pilgrimages, celebrations and festivals with offerings, from vodou festivals and neopagan conferences to Ancient Egyptian mystical days.

END OF JUNE/BEGINNING OF JULY

○ ✷ ◇ ***MATARIKI***

In Aotearoa (New Zealand), many Māori people celebrate the first rising of the star cluster Matariki (the Pleiades) in late June or early July as the start of the New Year, and it is now a public holiday. Over the course of several nights, people come outside to view the stars, make forecasts for the year to come and make food offerings to the cluster. According to Māori tradition, this consists of seven stars: the central star Matariki and her six children (though some texts refer to nine stars). It is a time to honour ancestors who have passed and think to the year ahead.

JULY

○ ✷ ◇ ***NIMAN***

Celebrated by the matrilineal Hopi in southwestern USA, this ceremony represents when the Kachina, supernatural spirits who visit Hopi villages for the first part of the year, return to their own homes in the mountains. The timings of the sixteen-day festival in July are determined by the position of the Sun and Moon each year. Masked dancers represent the Kachina, priests perform rain-making rituals and artists make ceremonial wooden Kachina dolls (*tihü*). Hopi people gather to say goodbye, feast and hope for a good summer harvest. It is also when newly married women are given robes by their husbands.

KEY ○ Historical Event ✷ Annual Event ◇ Variable Dates

14 TO 16 JULY

MIRACULOUS VIRGIN OF SAUT D'EAU & ÈZILI DANTÒ

Adherents of Haitian vodou make a pilgrimage to the waterfall of Saut d'Eau to honour the Miraculous Virgin, one of the lwa (spirits/deities) who is also venerated as Saint Anne (Mother of the Virgin Mary) or Little Saint Anne (Kreyol: Ti Sent Án). It is said that Èzili Dantò (Erzulie Dantor), also one of the lwa, appeared on a palm tree near the waterfall and healed the sick. Pilgrims take a purifying bath in the waterfall and bring offerings such as flowers, perfume or syrup, as well as herbs sacred to the Miraculous Virgin.

'Sèn Jak se Ogou, Ogou se dife.'

(Saint James is Ogou, Ogou is fire)

—Cultural and religious syncretism within Haitian vodou tradition

JULY

STARWOOD FESTIVAL

This American neopagan and New Age festival runs workshops on Tarot, Thelema, shamanism and Wicca, to name a few. Attendees can include the Church of All Worlds and the Druidic organization Ár nDraíocht Féin.

27 TO 31 JULY

EPAGOMENAL DAYS

These five days, in legend won by Thoth in a game with the moon god Khonsu, are regarded as a mystical 'days out of time' to honour several gods and bring the Ancient Egyptian calendar into line with the solar year. Hermetic practitioners apply them to the last few days of July, before the heliacal rising of Sopdet, or Sirius, relating to the historic annual inundation of the Nile. This is a time for attunement to each deity's energies and for healing:

- Ausar (Osiris) – 27 July
- Heru-Ur (Horus the Elder) – 28 July
- Set (Seth) – 29 July
- Aset (Isis) – 30 July
- Nebt-Het (Nephthys) – 31 July

'... when we look upon the Blazing Star, we are not gazing at ornament or allegory, but at the emblem of our ultimate destiny.'

—Alice Bailey, Occultist

RITUALS, SPELLS & DIVINATION

COURAGE & EMPOWERMENT SPELL

Spellwork for July focuses on gaining courage and empowerment once the month enters the zodiac sign of Leo, relying on this sunlit, fiery energy to drive magical work forwards and manifest positive abundance.

First, make some oil of borage (see page 126), a herb associated with courage, by placing a sprig in a small bottle of oil. Use this to anoint an orange candle, then place this on your altar (or another special space). Light it on a Sunday and visualize courage spreading out from the flame, filling you with the strength of a lion. ***Take care: borage is toxic if ingested.**

SIRIUS GATEWAY PATHWORK

The Sirius Gateway takes place around 7 July and is said to take the form of a high-frequency energetic gateway between Earth and the rising star Sirius, the Dog Star, into which one can tap to promote spiritual growth (see page 110).

For a Kabbalistic pathworking on or near the dates of the Gateway, imagine yourself taking the path from Yesod (the Moon) to Tiphareth (the Sun), also using the imagery of the Tarot's Major Arcana (see pages 188 and 189).

TAROT CORRESPONDENCE

The Sun card represents vitality and new life, and the suit of Wands relates to energy and fire. In the Tarot, Yesod (the lunar sphere) relates to the Nines, the suit of near-completion and integration. Tiphareth (the solar sphere) is connected in the Minor Arcana to the suit of the Sixes, which symbolizes balance, as well as to The Sun Tarot card.

NUMEROLOGY

Cancer's ruler, the Moon, is linked to the number 2, which represents receptivity, intuition and the unconscious. The number 7, connected to deep thought and the search for knowledge and wisdom, also has links to July.

CELESTIAL MAGIC

July sees a shift from Water and the zodiac sign of Cancer, to Fire and Leo, and the heliacal rising of the star Sirius, which has significance to many esoteric practitioners.

MOONS

July's Full Moon is called the Thunder Moon and the Hay Moon. Some Indigenous peoples from North America call it the Buck Moon since it is when deer begin to grow antlers.

METEOR SKIES

The Delta Aquariid meteor shower begins on 12 July, peaking on 28 and 29 July.

SIRIUS RISING

To many occultists, Sirius, the Dog Star, which rises in July, is the 'spiritual Sun', the light within the human soul. In Freemasonry,

The Anglo-Saxon Hay Moon

Sirius represents Divine Light, and derives from the Greek *seirios*, to mean 'blazing' or 'scorching'. In Ancient Egypt it was associated with the goddess Isis.

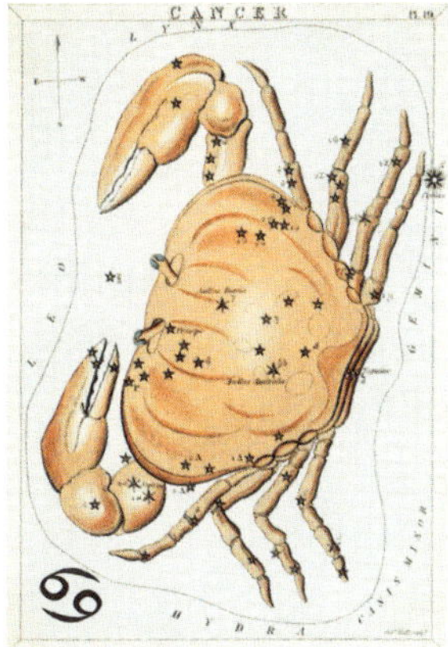

Water

Moon

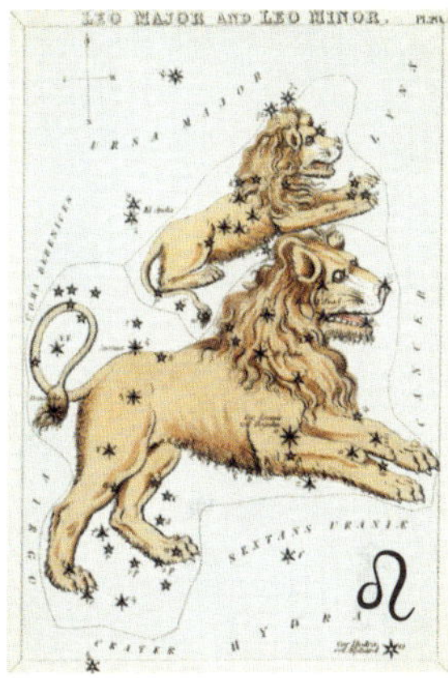

Fire

Sun

ELEMENTAL & ZODIAC CORRESPONDENCES

Water and the sign of Cancer preside over much of July, sliding into Fire and the energy of Leo towards month's end. Leo's constellation was thought to contribute to summer's intense heat, and the Ancient Egyptians revered it, believing its rising was connected with the annual rising of the Nile. Ancient Greeks saw it as the Nemean Lion, slain by Hercules, who used its skin as a cloak and placed it in the sky. Some knew it as the Star of Bacchus: Dionysus had the lion as his symbol and wore a lion's skin. Modern pagans link it with the Egyptian goddess Sekhmet.

PLANETARY CORRESPONDENCES

July is linked to the Moon and Sun. The Moon connects with Yesod (the lunar sphere) on the Kabbalistic Tree of Life, moving to Tiphareth (the solar sphere), further up the Tree's central pillar.

TAROT CORRESPONDENCES

Leo is linked to The Sun card, with its forceful solar energy, but also to the card of Strength, depicting a woman gently closing the jaws of a lion and symbolizing sustained, non-aggressive power. Leo is also connected to the fiery suit of Wands.

SYMBOLS

July's astrological symbols relate to Cancer, ♋, and the Moon, ☽, and also to Leo, ♌, and the Sun, ☉.

EARTHLY CONNECTIONS

Plants & Trees

CHAMOMILE (*MATRICARIA CHAMOMILLA*)

Esoteric Associations: protection, purification, sleep.

Uses: Chamomile can be burned in an incense in the home as a purifier, made into a floorwash or used in a ritual bath. It is said to have the power to break negative magic, including curses. It can also be made into a tea and drunk before or after rituals as a grounding measure.

LARKSPUR (*DELPHINIUM*)

Esoteric Association: wards off negative magic.

Uses: Larkspur is one of July's birth plants. Different coloured larkspur have different associations, ranging from deep blue (dignity) to white (purity and innocence). It is said to heal scorpion stings and guard against them. **Toxic: do not ingest.**

WATER LILY (*NYMPHAEACEAE*)

Esoteric Associations: joy, rebirth.

Uses: In contemporary magic within the Egyptian tradition, use blue lotus flowers in incense dedicated to the goddess Isis (see page 165), or in an oil for anointing. It is meant to enhance intuition and psychic powers. Water lily is July's second birth plant.

OAK (QUERCUS)

Esoteric Associations: strength, power, spiritual realm.

Uses: A carved acorn atop stair banisters is said to avert lightning strikes, while hanging one in a window can offer spiritual protection. The oak is the seventh tree (10 June–7 July, see page 187) in the Celtic tree calendar. Its Irish name, *duir*, refers to door: it is considered a doorway into the spiritual realm –and may relate to 'Druid'.

Gemstones

RUBY

Esoteric Associations: May birthstone, love, passion.

Uses: Can be effective as a talisman for courage in war, and as a protective charm.

AMBER

Esoteric Association: protection.

Uses: Can be worn as a protective charm, to ward off negative influence. Linked to the Sun – in folklore, some held it to be its fossilized rays.

Runes

FEHU ✦ 29 JUNE–14 JULY

F: Domestic cattle, wealth. This rune refers to wealth that must be guarded but not hoarded.

URUZ ✦ 14–29 JULY

U: Auroch, a wild ox. Relates to courage, endurance, energy and making our desires manifest.

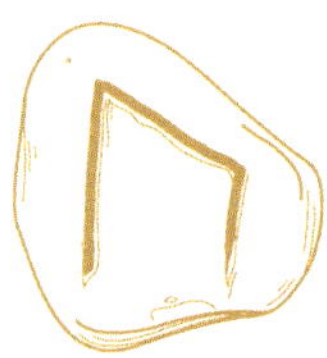

FOLKLORE & MYTH

ST SWITHUN'S DAY

In British folklore, if it rains on St Swithun's Day, 15 July, it will rain for forty days afterwards, whereas if not, it will be sunny for forty days. Legend states that when the remains of Saint Swithun (or Swithin), a ninth-century Anglo-Saxon bishop, were moved, there was a period of rain for forty days.

OYSTER DAY

Oysters are sometimes connected to St James's Feast Day on 25 July, a date that also traditionally heralds the beginning of oyster-fishing season. St James himself is often associated with shells, and grottos and shrines decorated with oyster and scallop shells were made on his day, often by children, with flowers, seaweed and lit candles out front.

SICURI/SIKURI

Originating in the Peruvian highlands, Sicuri is a collective dance form with a spiritual connection to the earth and the *apus* (mountain spirits). It is often performed during the festivals of patron saints and carnivals.

TANABATA

Japanese legend tells of smitten deities Hikoboshi (the cowherd star, Altair) and Orihime (the weaver star, Vega), forced apart by Orihime's father, yet for one night each year, on the seventh day of the seventh month (variable, but often 7 July or 7 August), they 'dance' together in the sky. On this eve, people celebrate with festivals, visit shrines and hang their wishes (*tanzaku*) on bamboo shoots. It may be connected to the Qixi Festival and legend in China (see page 128).

'Dog Days bright and clear indicate a happy year.'

—Folklore saying about the heliacal rising of Sirius, the Dog Star

Oyster Girl by Henry Robert Morland, 1797.

VIII

AUGUST

This month is known in modern paganism for the great harvest festival of Lughnasadh (Lammas), in which the god, having come to fruition in the form of the corn harvest, is ritually sacrificed: the song of John Barleycorn relates to this. The god, Lugh, is also celebrated at this time. The element of Fire changes to Earth, and the zodiac swings around to Virgo, a figure connected to the Classical grain goddesses of Ceres and Demeter, and to The Empress card of the Tarot.

THEMES & ENTITIES

August is a month of light and heat: although the year is turning darker after the Summer Solstice, the nights are still light and the days long. It is harvest time and the deities of this month reflect both the weather and the burgeoning crops.

LUGH

Irish deity Lugh of the Long Arm is the light-bringer, a god of the Sun and of summer, also connected with storms. In legend, his mother, Tailtiu, died of exhaustion after clearing the plains of Eire for crops – Lugh established the Tailteann Games (Óenach Tailten) in her memory. Held 1 August, it also included horse races, and was a popular time for handfastings (pagan marriages).

OPS

Ops – 'Plenty' – is an Ancient Greek goddess whose festival, the Opiconsivia, was celebrated on 25 August. Associated with Saturn, she is a harvest goddess, and an entity who resides underground.

DIANA

Huntress Diana is also a goddess of the Moon and of childbirth. A deity of the wild, she later became a patron of the 'tamed' countryside, and she has links to the crossroads, seen as a path to the Underworld: she thus has a chthonic nature as well as a lunar one. She is often represented as a triple goddess, symbolizing the Moon's phases, and is a protectress of women (see page 121).

HAMALIEL

ANGELIC CORRESPONDENCE

Hamaliel is the patron of logic and teaching and is associated with August. He is the ruler of Virgo, as mentioned in the *Three Books of Occult Philosophy* in the 1500s.

ASTAROTH

DEMONIC CORRESPONDENCE

Astaroth was described by occultist Francis Barrett as a Prince of Hell. Sixteenth-century demonologists state that his power is particularly strong in August.

SABBATS, FESTIVALS & CELEBRATIONS

August's heat, light and harvest set the tone for magical practice, empowerment, strength and gathering in.

1 AUGUST

○ ***LUGHNASADH / LAMMAS***

✷ This is a time of fertility, fruitfulness and celebration. Lughnasadh refers to the bright god Lugh (see page 118), whereas Lammas is said to come from the Anglo-Saxon *hlaef mass* or 'loaf mass', when the bread from the first wheat of the year was eaten.

This pagan festival has a darker side: that of sacrifice and death. The folk song 'John Barleycorn' sums this up – the corn is sown, sprouts, ripens and is harvested. It is this harvesting that represents the dark side of sacrifice. Today, it is celebrated with bonfires, a symbolic slaying of the god, and by decorating the house with corn dollies or sheaves of wheat. Bread is baked as a Lammas offering.

'We have ploughed, and we have sowed, We have reaped and we have mowed, And we have brought home every load. Hurrah for the Harvest Home!'

—Traditional English folk song 'Harvest Home'

KEY ○ Historical Event ✷ Annual Event ◇ Variable Dates

13 TO 15 AUGUST

NEMORALIA

This Ancient Roman festival to the hunting goddess of the Moon, Diana (see page 119), has been revived by some pagan groups. In the original, hunting dogs were garlanded with flowers and there was a parade around Lake Nemi near Rome to the shrine of the goddess. Now, celebrants might make small figures of wild animals as offerings. The Italian town of Nemi has started holding the festival again, this time as a cultural and historical celebration (without the ritual sacrifices).

14 TO 15 AUGUST

YAM FESTIVAL

In Benin, West Africa, the annual Yam Festival is celebrated by those who follow the region's Vodun religion. To ensure the new yam harvest, offerings are made to the following gods in propitiation: Heviosso (thunder and lightning); Sakpata (earth and smallpox); Azaka (agriculture); and Daah (rainbows and snakes).

END OF AUGUST

MA'NENE

The Toraja people of Sulawesi in Indonesia usually hold this three-day festival in August every three years. During the festival, the bodies of the dead are disinterred by relatives, and washed and dressed in fresh clothes. In local belief, ancestral spirits remain close to their families and must be honoured. Prior to this, the corpse is kept in the family home until relatives can afford a funeral, at which a water buffalo is sacrificed to give the deceased person a ride to the Otherworld. After this, the dead person is disinterred at Ma'nene. Food, drink and cigarettes may be offered to the deceased at this time.

LAST SATURDAY IN AUGUST

KULAMBA CEREMONY

Held by the Chewa people of Zambia, Malawi and Mozambique in Southern Africa, this ceremony features ritual dances and initiations by masked, ashen performers known as Nyau, who represent the spirit world and the departed.

RITUALS, SPELLS & DIVINATION

HARVEST SPELL

If wanted, cast your circle in the usual way (see page 189) and light a charcoal block for your incense and your candle. Choose one of the harvest goddesses or gods (Demeter, Kore, Ceridwen, the Dagda or the spirit of John Barleycorn) and raise the corn in turn. Thank the Lady of the Harvest for her bounty and abundance, and raise the bowl of grain. Raise the glass of wine and acknowledge that she takes, as well as gives. Spend your time within your circle doing what seems appropriate (prayer, a Tarot reading to divine the next six weeks, a dance) before closing.

For this, you will need:

- ✦ One yellow candle
- ✦ One bowl of spring water
- ✦ One bowl of corn
- ✦ One glass of red wine or grape juice
- ✦ Some Lughnasadh incense (a pinch each of frankincense, myrrh and rose petals)

SPELL TO MERCURY

If you are having communication issues, you may wish to undertake a petition to Mercury: light a yellow candle on your altar or special place on a Wednesday, sacred to Mercury, and ask the god for guidance. Be warned, however – occultist Aleister Crowley maintained that Mercury was the easiest god to offend, and the most difficult to appease.

HAZEL DIVINATION

Druids legendarily carried rods of hazel and one may see it as a divining rod for inspiration. To gather one, find a tree that has not yet borne fruit and cut a branch at sunrise with a sickle, on a Wednesday. Hazel twigs are also used in dowsing, and in Wales, a hazel hat (made of woven twigs) was said to grant your desire.

NUMEROLOGY

As Leo is ruled by the Sun, its number is 1, relating to independence, fresh starts and leadership.

Painting detail of *Landscape with Ceres (Allegory of Earth)* by Jan Brueghel the Younger and Hendrik van Balen, 1630s.

CELESTIAL MAGIC

Astrologically, the Sun in Leo – outgoing, grandiose and associated with the element of Fire – moves into Virgo's practicality, duty and its correspondence to the element of Earth.

MOONS

To some Indigenous peoples in North America, such as the Algonquin, the Full Moon in August is known as the Sturgeon Moon, but it is also known as the Grain Moon.

METEOR SKIES

The meteor shower of the Perseids, caused when Earth travels through comet debris, peaks around 12 August.

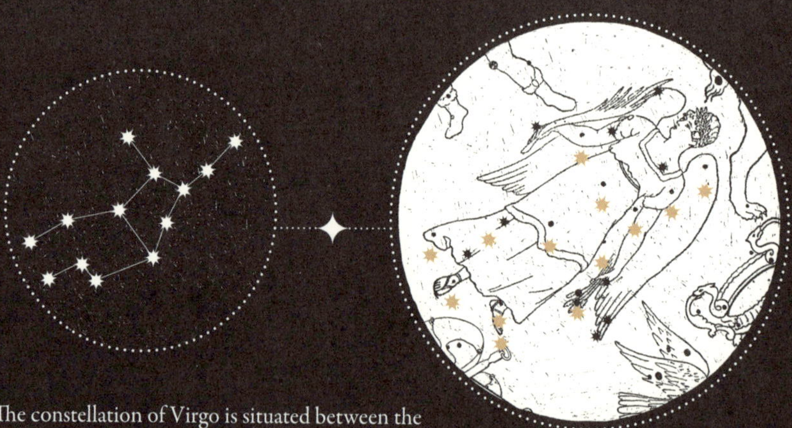

The constellation of Virgo is situated between the constellations Leo to its west and Libra to its east. Although located in the southern celestial hemisphere, it is a prominent feature in the Northern Hemisphere's spring and summer night sky.

ELEMENTAL & ZODIAC CORRESPONDENCES

August begins with Fire and Leo, before moving into Earth and Virgo's prosperity. Babylonians knew the Virgo constellation as the Furrow, depicting the goddess Šala with an ear of corn or barley. Later, the constellation was equated to the goddess Persephone, and to Astraea, the last of the Greek Immortals to leave Earth. The constellation is also linked to a cluster of grain and fertility goddesses – Spica, Virgo's principal star, means 'ear of grain'.

Fire

Sun

Earth

Mercury

PLANETARY CORRESPONDENCE

Virgo, ruled by Mercury, is associated with the Kabbalistic sephirah of Hod (Communication/Intellect) and the pathway between Chesed (Mercy/Kindness) and Tiphareth (Beauty/Balance).

TAROT CORRESPONDENCES

Virgo is linked to The Empress, and The Hermit, who represents introspection and is guided by his own inner light. The sephirah of Hod (see above) is associated with the Strength card.

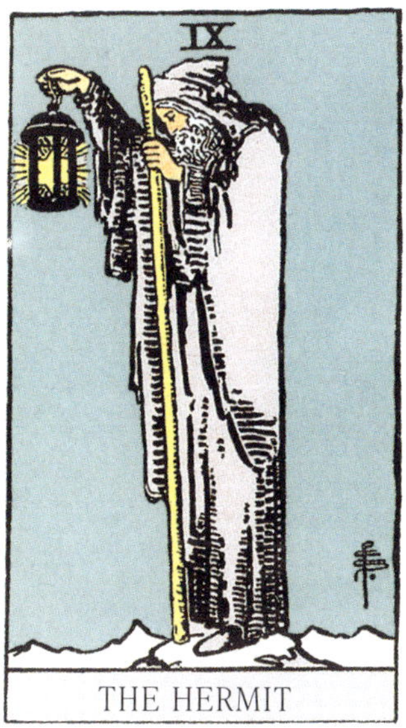

SYMBOLS

The astrological symbols for August relate to Leo, ♌, and the Sun, ☉, as well as to Virgo, ♍, and her ruler, Mercury, ☿.

EARTHLY CONNECTIONS

Plants & Trees

CALENDULA (*CALENDULA OFFICINALIS*)

Esoteric Associations: healing, the Sun.

Uses: It is considered an excellent medicinal remedy for burns – recalling the microcosm/macrocosmic theory linking it to the Sun (see page 11). In folklore, you are supposed to pick calendula (marigold) when the Sun enters the zodiac sign of Virgo.

BORAGE (*BORAGO OFFICINALIS*)

Esoteric Associations: strength, courage.

Uses: The Romans are said to have ingested it before heading into battle, though it is now known to be toxic and must not be consumed. Add to incense for strength, perhaps in difficult circumstances, or make an oil for a Courage & Empowerment Spell (see page 109). The Elizabethans held that it could lift melancholy. **Toxic: do not ingest.**

HOLLY (*ILEX AQUIFOLIUM*)

Esoteric Associations: fire, strength, protection.

Uses: Placing nine holly leaves under your pillow is thought to reveal your future partner in your dreams (see page 128).

HAZEL (CORYLUS AVELLANA)

Esoteric Associations: wisdom, divination, inspiration.

Uses: Sitting close to a hazel was held to promote good health. A double hazelnut (St John's nut) in one's pocket was once carried as a protective charm against toothache.

Gemstones

GREEN PERIDOT

Esoteric Association: protection.

Uses: Sometimes known as 'gem of the Sun', this was worn by Ancient Egyptian priests and was said to drive away evil spirits and night terrors.

SPINEL

Esoteric Associations: vitality, optimism.

Uses: Carry to enhance vitality and strength; connected in some traditions to the root chakra. Its red form is linked to passion.

SARDONYX

Esoteric Associations: protection, celestial influences.

Uses: Soldiers carried sardonyx into battle for protection and Ancient Egyptians used it in talismans and amulets.

Runes

THURISAZ ✦ 29 JULY–13 AUGUST

TH: Thorn or a Giant. A rune of raw power and energy on the physical plane; sometimes described as 'dangerous'.

ANSUZ ✦ 13–29 AUGUST

A: The As, ancestral god, i.e. Odin. A rune concerned with communication, language, wisdom and speech.

FOLKLORE & MYTH

DAY OF THE LADY OF HERBS & HARVEST/MATKA BOSKA ZIELNA

On 15 August, in Poland, many women gather herbs, such as tansy, mugwort (see page 70) and hyssop, in honour of the Assumption of the Virgin Mary. These herbs become wreaths or bundles to take to the church to be blessed: the herbs are then said to have protective powers, to be used in teas or to hang around the home.

PACHAMAMA RAYMI

The first of August sees the start of this festival in the Andes, with Altomisayoc (priests) honouring this ancient Earth goddess at the start of the Andean agricultural year. Offerings of food, alcohol, coca leaves and flowers are placed into a hole dug in the earth to thank the goddess for her bounty and protection. Ceremonial blankets are made and in Cusco, Peru, and people scatter yellow confetti and buy yellow flowers.

QIXI (七夕节)

Also known as 'Chinese Valentine's Day', this festival celebrates the legend of Niulang and Zhinü, who fall in love but are forbidden to marry because Niulang is not a god but an oxherd on Earth. Eventually the pair are reunited, but are separated by the Queen of Heaven and placed in the sky, with the Milky Way running between them. It is claimed that magpies build a bridge on the day of the festival to allow the separated lovers to meet (see also 'Tanabata', page 114).

HOLLY & HAZEL

The eighth tree in the Celtic tree calendar (8 July–4 Aug, see page 187), holly is linked to fire – the meaning of its Gaelic name, *tinne*, is 'iron bar' and it is ruled by Mars. Pliny mentions holly in Ancient Roman times as a protective tree, known to ward against evil magic and lightning. In Scotland, it is also thought to keep you safe from evil witches.

The hazel, with its quicksilver appearance, is linked to Mercury, and is the ninth tree in the Celtic tree calendar (5 Aug–1 Sept, see page 187). In both Welsh and Irish legend, hazelnuts fall into water, and are eaten by a magical or wise salmon. In the Irish version, they fall into Connla's Well, itself said to be under the sea, or in the Otherworld, and one suspects that the wisdom here is water wisdom, and the salmon's innate migratory knowledge.

'I went out to the hazel wood,
Because a fire was in my head,
And cut and peeled
a hazel wand,
And hooked a berry
to a thread;
And when white moths
were on the wing,
And moth-like stars were
flickering out,
I dropped the berry in a stream
And caught a little
silver trout.'

—*The Song of Wandering Aengus,* William Butler Yeats

IX

SEPTEMBER

Known to the Anglo-Saxons as *Gerst Monath* (Barley Month) or *Haefest Monath* (Harvest Month), September is when the Autumn Equinox falls. It is a time of Libran balance, when summer's energy and golden days gently wind down and autumn's colder weather starts to make its presence felt. Magically, it is a time to complete projects after the harvest and prepare for the darker part of the year, tidying up any loose ends.

THEMES & ENTITIES

Many of September's deities are, like those of August, harvest deities – but as the crops are gathered in, the gods and goddesses of this time start to become more chthonic as the year turns down towards the dark.

DEMETER

Demeter is the Greek goddess of corn and fertility. After her daughter, Persephone, was abducted to the Underworld by Hades, she allowed Earth's vegetation to die and winter to slide in while she initially searched for her child. Persephone was finally allowed to return to Earth, but only for half of each year, when Demeter's joy brings in the spring and summer.

PERSEPHONE

Demeter's daughter is strongly connected to ancient rites known as the Eleusinian mysteries. These are held in the month of Boedromion, which straddles September and October, and seem to have featured a re-enactment of Persephone's abduction by Hades to the Underworld, where she was forced to spend six months of every year after his trickery. Her release from the Underworld each year heralds spring.

BAIDI

The Chinese god of metal and autumn, Baidi is also known as the White Emperor and is a manifestation of the deity Shangdi. He is linked to the planet Venus.

ARCHANGEL MICHAEL

ANGELIC CORRESPONDENCE

Michael is the dragon slayer, who also combats Lucifer and in Hermetic and ceremonial traditions is linked to the south. His feast day is 29 September (see page 143).

HADAKIEL (CHEDEQIEL)

DEMONIC CORRESPONDENCE

Associated with the sign of Libra and with no fixed physical description, Hadakiel is often associated instead with symbols such as scales, sigils or even colours. His name possibly derives from 'Thorn of God'.

SABBATS, FESTIVALS & CELEBRATIONS

September is the golden month when the year begins to turn into its darker half after the Summer Equinox, a time for quiet reflection now that the summer has ended.

AUGUST OR SEPTEMBER

○ ✳ ◇ ***HUNGRY GHOST FESTIVAL/ ZHONGYUAN JIE***

In China, the seventh lunar month in the Chinese lunar calendar is called 'Ghost Month'. Somewhat similar to Samhain, this festival honours the ancestors. The gates of the Underworld are supposed to open at this time so that restless spirits return to the world and haunt the living. Food is given to them in offerings and paper items and joss sticks are burned so that they re-enter the Underworld and are received by the ancestors. Paper lanterns may be released upon water to light the spirits' way.

AROUND 21 SEPTEMBER

○ ✳ ◇ ***AUTUMN EQUINOX / MABON***

The year is once again in balance, with day and night of equal length. However, it is also when the tides of the year are on the change. In the Northern Hemisphere, the tides are ebbing rather than rising, and taking anything unwanted with them. Thus it is a good time to release anything for which you have no further need, and to celebrate the harvest that the year has brought – you can also regard it as the Harvest Home, a traditional English harvest festival. As at Lughnasadh (Lammas), you could bake bread to celebrate the festival, perhaps in the shape of a corn plait, or decorate the house with bunches of autumn leaves.

KEY ○ Historical Event ✳ Annual Event ◇ Variable Dates

The Autumn Equinox is sometimes called 'Mabon' by modern pagans. The name comes from the young god in Welsh legends, the son of the Modron (the names mean 'son' and 'mother'). The Mabon goes missing, and his frantic mother searches for him, enlisting the help of various people such as King Arthur's knights and the eldest animals and birds of Britain. In this, the story resembles the Greek myth of Persephone. But we should note that 'Mabon' is a recent name, conferred by writer Aiden Kelly in the 1970s, and there is no older textual connection between the Mabon in legend and the Autumn Equinox.

25 SEPTEMBER

ROI WANGOL

This vodou festival in Haiti honours the lwa Roi Wangol, who represents the force of the Sun. He is sometimes depicted as an old man who marries the Moon.

'Hoof and horn,
Hoof and horn
All that dies
shall be reborn
Corn and grain,
Corn and grain
All that falls shall
rise again
Sage and Crone,
Sage and Crone
Wisdom's gift shall
be our own
Crone and Sage,
Crone and Sage
Wisdom is the
gift of age'

—Modern pagan
and Wiccan chant

RITUALS, SPELLS & DIVINATION

FRUITFULNESS RITUAL

This ritual celebrates the arrival of the apples, in this season of 'mists and mellow fruitfulness' as noted in *Ode to Autumn* by John Keats.

For this, you will need:

- One black candle
- One white candle
- Your magical implements
- A bowl of water
- Three apples and some grain

Cast your circle and call the quarters (see page 189). You may wish to send prayers to Pomona, the Roman goddess of apples, or Cerridwen, the Welsh goddess of the harvest (see pages 160 and 104). Close your eyes and imagine the goddesses Pomona in the depths of an orchard, or Cerridwen in a cornfield, standing by the last sheaf of grain, left for luck by the harvesters. In the golden autumn light, the air smells of apples and smoke. Thank the goddess for her gifts and her guidance.

PATHWORKING & TAROT

If you would like to celebrate the Autumn Equinox as a point of balance, imagine the year as it turns: seeing it as a great wheel, around which the seasons are arranged (see page 14). Close your eyes and try to sense this day as a moment of perfect balance. Perhaps you can work with your guide or deity to gain more balance in your own life if you feel that you need it, or undertake a meditation or pathworking with the Tarot card of Justice, which is associated with the zodiac sign of Libra.

NUMEROLOGY

The ruler of Virgo, Mercury, is linked with the number 5, which represents knowledge, intelligence and understanding.

Vertumnus and Pomona by Francesco Melzi, 1518–1522. Pomona, the goddess of fruits and orchards, is visited by the god of seasons, Vertumnus, who has transformed himself into an old woman to enter her orchard and win her heart.

CELESTIAL MAGIC

September is all about balance, with the arrival of the Autumn Equinox around 21 September, when the Sun crosses the celestial equator, and the zodiac shifts from grounding Virgo into the more expansive sign of Libra, the Scales.

MOONS

The Full Moon of September, often very low, large and deep golden, is called the Harvest Moon, Full Corn Moon and the Celtic Vine Moon (or Muin); it is associated with the autumn harvest and the Autumn Equinox (Mabon).

METEOR SKIES

The meteor shower of the Epsilon Perseids, from the Perseus constellation, peaks every year around 9 September and is best viewed after midnight or in areas of low light pollution.

Harvest Moon

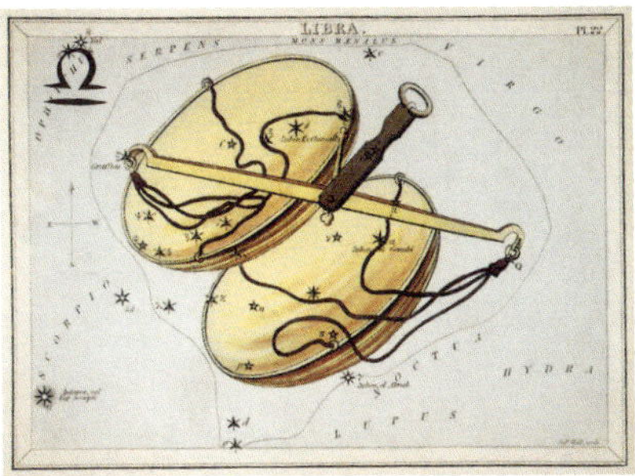

Air Venus

ELEMENTAL & ZODIAC CORRESPONDENCES

As the zodiac sign of Virgo moves into Libra towards September's end, we shift from Earth to Air. The grounding of magical practices from the first part of September is now rooted, leaving the practitioner free to move into Air's liberating qualities. The principal star of Libra's constellation is Zubenelgenubi, the 'southern claw'; accompanying stars

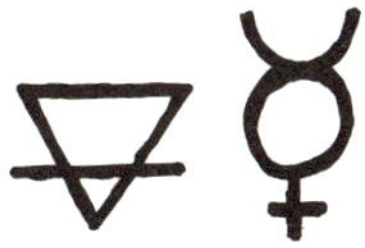

Earth Mercury

are Zubeneschamali, the 'northern claw' and Zubenelakrab, the 'scorpion's claw'. This constellation was known to the Babylonians as the Scales, sacred to the god of justice, Shamash; to the Greeks and Arabs it was called the Scorpion's Claws. Autumn's arrival is heralded by the Great Square of Pegasus, marked by the stars Scheat, Alpheratz, Markab and Algenib.

PLANETARY CORRESPONDENCES

Virgo is ruled by Mercury, and Libra by Venus (linked to the Kabbalistic sephirah of Netzach – love and intuition).

TAROT CORRESPONDENCES

The Roman goddess Justitia (associated with Libra and the Scales) appears in the Justice card, not blindfolded as can be typical, but staring directly outwards.

SYMBOLS

The astrological symbols for September relate to Virgo, ♍, and Mercury, ☿, as well as to Libra, ♎, and her ruler, Venus, ♀.

EARTHLY CONNECTIONS

Plants & Trees

VINE (*VITIS VINIFERA*)

Esoteric Associations: fruitfulness, intuition, instinct.

Uses: Although *muin* refers to the vine in the Ogham tree alphabet, it can also refer to the bramble. It is tenth in the Celtic tree calendar (2–29 Sept, see page 187). Vine is linked to Dionysus, the lionskin-clad god of the vine and the grape, whose gifts can display a darker side if they are abused. In the tree alphabet, muin suggests that we need temporarily to bypass the rational mind and rely on the intuition and instinct. The vine represents fruitfulness and fertility. Its long tendrils reach out, suggesting a seeking to learn and understand. The old Irish name for the vine is 'strongest of effort': the vine seeks support and to climb high.

SAGE (*SALVIA OFFICINALIS*)

Esoteric Associations: cleanser, purifier, wisdom.

Uses: In European tradition, sage is sacred to Jupiter and its element is Air, which connects us to September and Libra. It is used in rituals to gain wisdom and its properties can be called upon to enhance one's understanding. Modern pagans have adopted the use of smudge (white sage), a historic practice by Indigenous peoples in North and South America, as a means of cleansing rooms before or during ritual (see page 189).

ROSEMARY (*ROSMARINUS OFFICINALIS*)

Esoteric Associations: cleansing, protection.

Uses: Keep sprigs of it in the house to clear the space and its fresh, astringent scent will remind you of fresh starts.

Gemstones

SAPPHIRE

Esoteric Associations: loyalty, wisdom, healing.

Uses: September birthstone; in ancient Persia, there was a belief that the sky rested upon a huge sapphire, hence its colour. In medieval times, it was thought to cure diseases, especially those of the eye, and boils caused by the plague. It was also said to act as an antidote to poison.

LAPIS LAZULI

Esoteric Associations: strength, deity.

Uses: September birthstone; it has close associations with Ancient Egypt, whose people believed that the hair and eyebrows of the gods were made from it. A symbol of strength, it was linked with the dark blue of the night sky and its goddess, Nuit. It is said to promote the work of the higher mind.

Runes

RAIDHO ✦ 29 AUGUST–13 SEPTEMBER

R: Wagon or chariot. Represents physical or emotional journeys, advancing, leadership, good counsel, integrity.

KENAZ ✦ 13–28 SEPTEMBER

K: Beacon or torch. A rune of magic, and of shedding light, suggesting that things are about to be revealed.

Bromley Horn Dance

FOLKLORE & MYTH

BROMLEY HORN DANCE
Held on Wakes Monday (following the first Sunday after 4 September) in Abbots Bromley, Staffordshire, UK, this event involves six 'deer men', plus a Fool, a Hobby horse and Maid Marian, who undertake a dance with antlers that are kept in the local church. The dance is very old, dating at least to medieval times.

CHUSEOK (추석)
This annual Korean harvest festival with roots in shamanic traditions takes place in late September, but may occur in October as well because it is a lunisolar event. Offerings, known as *charye*, are given to honour the ancestors.

SHUBUN NO HI (秋分の日)
Ancestors and nature are venerated at this Japanese Equinox festival, which takes place on 22 or 23 September. Families take time to visit their relatives' graves and provide offerings and flowers. People often eat a sticky rice treat called *ohagi*.

MICHAELMAS DAY
29 September is dedicated to St Michael (see page 133) and marks the end of the summer and the start of the autumn: hiring fairs and the start of the academic term begin now. Traditionally, you are supposed to eat goose today to bring luck.

ROSEMARY LEGEND
Commonly said to be an aid to divining your future partner, this herb is associated with the love goddess, Aphrodite (see page 62). Plant sprigs in separate pots and attach a name to each one: the plant that grows the strongest holds the name of the one you should marry. Seventeenth-century herbalist Culpeper refers to it as a 'sovereign balm'. In medieval times, it was associated with love and memory, and could be thrown into graves as a sign that the dead would be remembered. Greek scholars are said to have worn a sprig of rosemary as an aid to mental concentration and intellectual acuity.

'Rosemarie, that's for remembrance...'

—Shakespeare's Ophelia

X

OCTOBER

The name *October* is Latin and means 'eighth', but in Welsh it is called *Hydref* – the word for autumn itself. The Anglo-Saxons named it *Winterfylleth* ('winter is coming'). It carries the weight of endings and the mystery of what lies beyond, as the Wheel of the Year turns towards Samhain, the festival of spirits and the dead. October is a potent time for divination, for returning to the old customs of folklore, shadow work and connecting with hidden knowledge.

THEMES & ENTITIES

October is a calm time after harvest, offering an opportunity for reflection before the closely related festivals of Samhain and Hallowe'en. It is a month in which many traditions remember the dead and venerate the ancestors, when letting go seems natural as the leaves fall from the trees and the nights become longer and colder.

HECATE/HEKATE

Honoured at Samhain and throughout October by many pagans, Hecate is a Greek goddess of the Underworld (her origins might be Anatolian). She is found at the crossroads, with her faithful dogs by her side. But despite these chthonic origins, she is also linked to children and childbirth – many women died in childbirth prior to modern medicine. In Ptolemaic Alexandria, she was also linked to witchcraft, ghosts and curses. Meat was left as an offering to her, and sometimes dogs were sacrificed. The writer Athenaeus states that the red mullet is sacred to her, as the fish is blood-coloured, and will eat corpses. Poisons such as aconite, dittany, mandrake and belladonna (see page 154) are linked to her, as is the cypress (a funerary tree) and yew (see page 155).

THE CAILLEACH

This goddess is traditionally seasonal, emerging with the first cold winds of winter. She is known in Scotland as 'the breath of the Cailleach Bheaur', the blue hag of winter. In Scottish folklore the Cailleach wakes every Samhain, bringing gales, snow and cold weather before turning to stone at Imbolc in February. Her name means 'older wise woman' in Gaelic.

BARBIEL

ANGELIC CORRESPONDENCE

As the ruling power of Scorpio, Barbiel is linked with truth and justice. Sometimes depicted with roses, he is the patron of converts.

BAAL

DEMONIC CORRESPONDENCE

Baal is a King of Hell and one of the first spirits summoned in the *Lesser Key of Solomon*. He is sometimes depicted as a triple figure composed of a man, a cat and a toad, and is said to be able to confer the power of invisibility. His power is supposed to be strongest in October.

SABBATS, FESTIVALS & CELEBRATIONS

Towards the end of October, the pagan and occult worlds celebrate the great festivals of the dead, such as Samhain and Hallowe'en, commensurate with the Underworld and the ancestral nature of this month.

SEPTEMBER OR OCTOBER

○ ✷ ◇ ***CHANG'E***

This Chinese moon goddess's festival takes place in either September or October, depending on the lunar calendar. In legend, Chang'e is a mortal woman and the wife of a renowned archer. In some versions of her story, she steals a magic potion from her husband and drinks it, becoming immortal and flying to the Moon with her pet rabbit, who can still be seen in the Moon today (see Hare Lore, page 59). To help celebrate her legend, people spend time with their families, view the Full Moon and eat mooncakes.

'Chang'e must regret having stolen the elixir of life, as she gazes at the emerald sea and blue sky night after night.'

—*Chang'e*, a poem by Li Shangyin (Tang Dynasty)

KEY ○ Historical Event ✷ Annual Event ◇ Variable Dates

31 OCTOBER TO 1 NOVEMBER

SAMHAIN

There's very little evidence that the ancient Celts regarded this festival as the start of the New Year, as modern pagans do now, but it may have been a festival based on the slaughter of cattle for the winter season. Many pagans use this dark time to honour their ancestors, and those who have died in the previous year. Modern witches often hold a Dumb Supper: a place is laid at a table for everyone who has died in the previous year, and the living have their supper in silence, honouring the memories of those who have died.

31 OCTOBER

NOS CALAN GAEAF

In Wales, the eve of Calan Gaeaf (the first day of winter) is an *Ysbrydnos*: a time when spirits are abroad and people must avoid churchyards and other places where spirits might gather (see page 156). Historically, men would dress up in a pig's skin, or dress as *gwrachod* (hags or witches) and go from house to house, begging for food, drink or coins.

31 OCTOBER

HALLOWE'EN

Hallowe'en is host to a variety of customs, including trick-or-treating and pumpkin carving. In the UK, these would originally have been turnip lanterns, carved with alarming faces to frighten away evil spirits, but pumpkins have become more common. Children often dress up as ghosts, witches or other scary figures.

31 OCTOBER

OICHE SHAMHNA

In Ireland, on Oiche Shamhna (Samhain Eve), spirits are held to walk at this time, which is also known as Puca (Goblin) Night. In older times, bonfires were lit in the evening to provide protection against malevolent spirits. Food and drink offerings were left outside homes, in hopes to appease wandering souls, while people donned disguises to blend in with the spirits, a practice that evolved into modern Hallowe'en costumes.

RITUALS, SPELLS & DIVINATION

SAMHAIN RITUAL

On 31 October, honour Samhain with a bonfire or a circle of candles. Write down habits or thoughts you wish to release, then safely burn the paper, symbolizing transformation. Close the ritual by setting intentions for the months ahead.

ANCESTOR ALTARS

This is an ideal time for introspection, ancestral connection and transformative rituals. You can create an altar dedicated to your ancestors, with photos, heirlooms, candles and offerings such as food or drink. Light candles in their honour and meditate, focusing on gratitude and guidance. This practice strengthens the ancestral bond and invites wisdom from the past. Many practitioners perform rites of release, burning a written wish in a ritual fire (see safe fire use, page 189). Group gatherings may involve meditative walks, shared feasts and communal ceremonies. Some people make soul cakes to give to visitors, following the old custom of 'souling'.

DIVINATION

Use Tarot, runes or scrying (see pages 187–89) to seek guidance from the spirit realm. To dream of the future, cut ten leaves of ivy, throw one away and put the other nine under your pillow. In Scotland and Wales, white stones were placed within a bonfire, marked for each person: if any were missing in the morning, those people would die within the year. In northern England, on 'Nut-crack Night', hazelnuts were cast into the fire for the purposes of divination. In apple bobbing, the first to bite into a bobbing apple would be the first to marry.

HALLOWE'EN LANTERNS

Place a Hallowe'en pumpkin or turnip lantern on a windowsill facing outwards to scare away any negative energies.

NUMEROLOGY

The number of October is 6, relating to Venus, the ruler of Libra, and thus to love, beauty and fertility.

Snap-Apple Night by Daniel Maclise, 1833. People engaging in traditional divination games and feasting in celebration of Samhain.

CELESTIAL MAGIC

October sees Air shifting into Water with the advent of Scorpio. Alchemically, this time of year represents *nigredo*, the blackening phase of decay – reflecting the shadow aspects of Scorpio and Pluto.

MOONS

The time of the Hunter's Moon – in its light, people could hunt more effectively. The Anglo-Saxons called it *Winterfylleth*, like the month. Known as Dying Grass Moon or Blood Moon amongst some Native American peoples, it symbolized a time of vegetation dying back and hunting becoming necessary.

METEOR SKIES

This is a key time of the year for meteor showers. The Draconids peak around 8 October and the Orionids peak around 21 to 22 October.

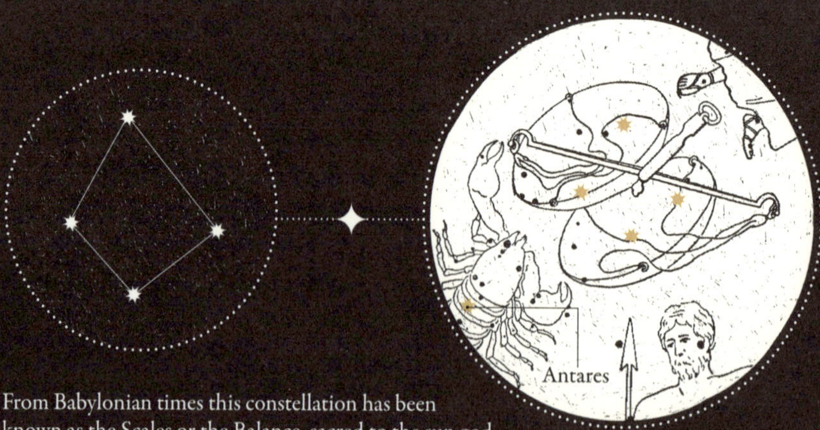

From Babylonian times this constellation has been known as the Scales or the Balance, sacred to the sun god Shamash (patron of truth and justice), and marking the time of equal day and night. The stars also formed the claws of the Scorpion but the Romans separated Libra from Scorpius, creating it as its own constellation.

ELEMENTAL & ZODIAC CORRESPONDENCES

October is first associated with Air, the element linked to its principal zodiac sign of Libra, then to Water and Scorpio, which enters around the 23rd of the month. Scorpio is also a constellation, containing the red star Antares. In Egypt, Antares featured in religious ceremonies. It is probably associated with Isis, and with the scorpion goddess Selket. Called 'the great beast' and the 'great sign' by early astronomers, it was seen as a constellation of darkness and endurance by Mesopotamians.

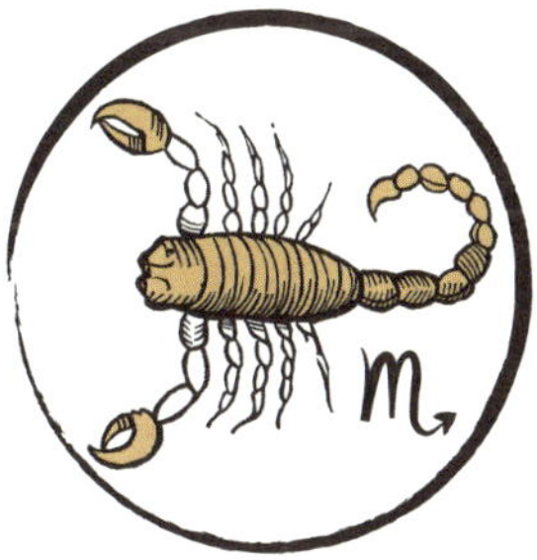

PLANETARY CORRESPONDENCES

Scorpio is ruled traditionally by Mars, but its modern ruler is said to be Pluto, which is related to death, transformation and change. On the Kabbalistic Tree of Life, Scorpio is connected to the path between Tiphareth and Netzach.

TAROT CORRESPONDENCES

Scorpio is associated with change, the Underworld and the Tarot card of Death, which relates to personal transformation.

SYMBOLS

The astrological symbols for October relate to Libra, ♎, and its ruler Venus, ♀, as well as to Scorpio, ♏, Mars, ♂, and Pluto, ♇.

EARTHLY CONNECTIONS

Plants & Trees

BELLADONNA (*ATROPA BELLADONNA*)

Esoteric Associations: spirit work, divination.

Uses: **Highly toxic** and historically used in flying ointments by witches, belladonna (deadly nightshade) is linked to explorations of the shadow self and connection with the unseen. It's not used physically in modern practices but holds powerful symbolic resonance.

WORMWOOD (*ARTEMISIA ABSINTHIUM*)

Esoteric Associations: spirit communication, banishing.

Uses: Traditionally used to open channels to the spirit world, wormwood is often included in incense blends for Samhain. It's believed to ward off evil spirits and negative energies. **Toxic: do not ingest.**

IVY (*HEDERA*)

Esoteric Associations: persistence, tenacity.

Uses: Eleventh in the Celtic tree calendar (30 Sept–27 Oct, see page 187), ivy gives clear insight and the means to cut through tangles to perceive the truth beneath. It can also refer to the spiral of the self, the quest for the inner self amongst one's psychological snarls. But be careful that you do not bind yourself to outworn ideas or emotions, as ivy can cling to a surface, ultimately destroying it. Call upon the imagery of ivy to navigate difficult situations.

YEW (*TAXUS BACCATA*)

Esoteric Associations: death, rebirth, immortality.

Uses: Yew trees have long been symbols of death and the afterlife in Druidic and other esoteric traditions. The tree's branches are used decoratively on ancestral altars to honour the cycle of life and death. **Toxic: do not ingest.**

Gemstone

OBSIDIAN

Esoteric Associations: protection, grounding.

Uses: Carrying a piece of obsidian with you is said to banish any negative influences.

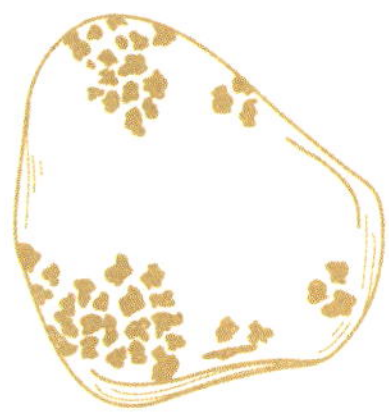

Runes

GEBO ✦ 28 SEPTEMBER–13 OCTOBER

G: Gift. This is a rune of balance, but can indicate that things are imbalanced or out of sync. The idea behind it is that if a gift is given, one should be returned. It relates also to legal matters.

WUNJO ✦ 13–28 OCTOBER

W or V: Joy. Happiness, contentment and joy! Envisage Wunjo in order to bring about a desired outcome.

FOLKLORE & MYTH

THINNING OF THE VEIL

The concept of the veil between the worlds of the living and the dead thinning at this time is sometimes held to come from Celtic beliefs, but it is more likely to have entered occult awareness in Europe from Theosophy, and Plutarch's description of a goddess statue in the city of Sais, inscribed: 'I am all that has been and is and shall be; and no mortal has ever lifted my mantle.' The mantle, or veil, represents the membrane between a superficial and perhaps profane apprehension of the mortal world, and the deeper understanding of the concealed world of nature. In the late seventeenth century, Enlightenment illustrations of Isis and her veil became increasingly common. Helena Blavatsky's important work *Isis Unveiled*, published in 1877, also brought the idea further into esoteric consciousness.

KANNAZUKI

In much of Japan, October is the 'month without gods' (*kannazuki*) – when all the gods are held to travel to Izumo for their annual meeting (hence the 'month with gods' – *kamiarizuki* – in Izumo itself).

CALAN GAEAF

This first day of winter in Wales reveals a number of spirits, including Y Ladi Wen (The White Lady), associated with graveyards and crossroads. She was believed to be a harbinger of death and would sometimes lure the unwary to her by offering treasure. Yr Hwch Ddu Gwta (The Black Sow) was said to chase people on Samhain, and children were warned that she would catch the last child home.

THE SLUAGH

In the Scottish Highlands and Islands in the nineteenth century, the Sluagh were supposed to be 'the spirits or mortals who had died'. Folklorist Alexander Carmichael was told on the Isle of Barra that these spirits fought battles in the air and that 'their crimson blood may be seen staining rocks and stones'. The Sluagh sometimes also took the form of vicious gusts of wind that burned the skin, or monstrous birds.

OLD MICHAELMAS DAY

Don't pick blackberries after 10 October – the Devil is said to urinate on them!

The monstrous birds of the Sluagh

XI

NOVEMBER

November is the quiet month, the pause in the year when the nights are darkest and longest in the approach to December's Winter Solstice. It is often when the first frosts occur and winter feels as though it has truly begun. It is, for many, a time for remembrance, reflection and commemoration. To the Anglo-Saxons, it was 'Blood Month,' *Blōtmōnaþ*, when animals were sacrificed for the winter.

THEMES & ENTITIES

November is the month in which preparation for midwinter and its great festivals are well underway. The entities of this month are those of late harvest and still, after Samhain, of death.

POMONA

A dryad and the goddess of orchard fruits and gardens, Pomona was celebrated by the Romans on 1 November, when the harvest was ripe. Nuts and apples were offered to her on this day. She is said to have rejected Vertumnus, a deity of seasonal change, until he gained entrance by devious means (see page 136).

HATHOR

Hathor is the cow-headed goddess of love and motherhood. As Mistress of the West, she welcomes the dead into their new life, and she assists women in childbirth. She is also known as Mehturt, meaning 'great flood', a reference to the Milky Way and to the rising of the Nile. Ra sent Hathor (as the avenging lioness, Sekhmet) to punish uprising humans.

BARON SAMEDI

In vodou traditions, Baron Samedi is said to be the spirit of the first man ever buried in a graveyard. He is often depicted as a skeleton, with outrageous, flamboyant behaviour and plenty of rude jokes. He is married to Maman Brigitte, a powerful lwa. His offerings include cigars and rum and he symbolizes resurrection.

ADNACHIEL

ANGELIC CORRESPONDENCE

This angel of Sagittarius represents independence and truth seeking.

ASMODEUS

DEMONIC CORRESPONDENCE

In the *Ars Goetia* grimoire, Asmodeus is depicted as 'having 3 heads: the first is like a bull, the second like a man, and the third like a ram or a goat; the tail of a serpent, and from his mouth issue flames of fire'. A demon of lust and revenge, his power is said to be strong in November.

SABBATS, FESTIVALS & CELEBRATIONS

Many November feasts of the dead take place around the first of November, with the Night of Hecate and World Occult Day taking place mid-month.

LATE OCTOBER TO EARLY NOVEMBER

○ ✷ ◇ *THE ISIA*

This festival of the goddess Isis was celebrated by the Romans. In Egypt, a festival honouring the myth of Osiris was held around the same time: it is unclear if they were connected. Osiris is one of the oldest known gods, with records dating back 2,500 years (see pages 165 and 170). The Greeks identified him with Hades, and with Dionysus. He is a lord of the Underworld and of death, but also of growth: it is probable that he began as a god of vegetation. The annual flooding of the Nile was attributed to him (he is connected to the constellation Orion, the rise of which is linked to the historic changes of the Nile).

1 NOVEMBER

○ ✷ *FÈT GEDE*

This Haitian vodou festival is linked to All Saints/All Souls, since it is a veneration of the Gede, the ancestors. Port-o-Prince has a large parade at this time, featuring spirit possession and visits to cemeteries. The dead are honoured with combinations of alcohol and hot peppers, and other offerings are made to their graves such as corn and coffee. The lwa spirit Baron Samedi (see page 161) presides over proceedings in his characteristic top hat and sunglasses.

KEY ○ Historical Event ✷ Annual Event ◇ Variable Dates

'Más sabe el diablo por viejo que por diablo.'
The devil knows more by being old than by being the devil.

—Saying, from The Day of the Dead, Mexico

1 NOVEMBER

THE DAY OF THE DEAD (DÍA DE LOS MUERTOS)

In a similar vein, Día de los Muertos is celebrated in Mexico, a combination of Catholic festivals and, according to some, ancient Aztec rites. *Calaveras* (sugar skulls) are made and altars are built to honour the ancestors. Marigolds are given as offerings. This is a celebratory festival with many light-hearted elements, such as comic epitaphs.

16 OR 17 NOVEMBER

THRACIAN NIGHT OF HECATE

This is still celebrated by some pagan communities. Offerings such as eggs, wine and keys are made at nearby crossroads on this night, when the Ancient Greek goddess of the Underworld, Hecate (see page 146) – often associated with witchcraft, ghosts, crossroads and curses – is said to walk the Earth.

18 NOVEMBER

WORLD OCCULT DAY

World Occult Day invites us to explore the mysteries of the occult world: of divination, the mystical and ritual. Its origins remain unclear, as befits the meaning of the word 'occult' – hidden or secret lore, relating to the supernatural realms.

'I am the Ancient
Apple Qyeen,
As once I was
so am I now.
For ever more
a hope unseen,
Betwix the blossom
and the bow.'

—William Morris

RITUALS, SPELLS & DIVINATION

ALL SOULS' DAY

This is part of the Allhallowtide season, during which prayers for the dead are said on 2 November in the Catholic tradition. Candles are lit to honour the dead and to ward away demons and evil, and graves are cleaned. Some pagans make soul cakes, a spiced, round shortbread. You may also undertake a Tarot reading at this time for the six weeks between Samhain and the Winter Solstice, or Yule.

RITUAL FOR POMONA

To honour Pomona (see page 160), on 1 November, place a bowl of apples and a bowl of earth upon your altar or in a special place. Light a green candle and make the following invocation (from modern Neo-Roman group Nova Roma): 'Pomona Dea, te hoc ture ommovendo bonas preces precor, uti sies volens propitia mihi et Senatui Populoque Novaromanorum Quiritum.' / 'Goddess Pomona, by offering this incense to you I pray good prayers, so that you may be willingly propitious to me and the Senate and People of the New Romans'.

ISIS & OSIRIS TEMPLE INCENSE

Since this was the period of the Isia, you can set up an altar with images of Isis and Osiris. Light a green candle for Osiris and a white one for Isis, and burn kyphi, the sacred incense of the Ancient Egyptians, who were said to burn it at dusk.

Mix the following together in a bowl:

- One tablespoon juniper berries
- One teaspoon raisins steeped in wine for three days and three nights
- One teaspoon each of: acacia leaves, henna, calamus root, mastic, peppermint, bay leaves, hibiscus, cinnamon, galangal, orris root, sandalwood
- Add powdered myrrh and honey to bind (don't use too much honey!), then dry on a baking sheet.

NUMEROLOGY

The number of November is 9, relating both to Mars and Pluto, the traditional and modern rulers of Scorpio and representing courage, passion and independence.

CELESTIAL MAGIC

In November, celestial work revolves around the shift from Scorpio and the element of Water to Sagittarius and the element of Fire, along with the build of power towards the Winter Solstice.

MOONS

November's Full Moon is known as the Beaver Moon – when beavers build their dams for the winter, and Indigenous peoples in North America hunted them for their fur. It is also known as the Ice Forming Moon (Ojibwe), when lakes and rivers freeze. In Celtic traditions the last Full Moon before the Winter Solstice is the Mourning Moon, believed to be a period when the boundary between the living world and the spirit world is thin.

METEOR SKIES

The Leonids – associated with the comet Tempel-Tuttle – are visible this month.

Beaver Moon

ELEMENTAL & ZODIAC CORRESPONDENCES

Early November is ruled by the element of Water and the sign of Scorpio, but towards the end of the month, this shifts to the element of Fire as we enter the sign of Sagittarius, the archer. Sagittarius, the constellation, is depicted as a centaur drawing a bow, with the arrow pointed at Antares, the heart of Scorpio. In Babylonia, this figure was said to be the winged god Nergal, and it was later associated with the Greek Chiron, the healer-centaur who is mistakenly slain by the hero Hercules. In Sumer, the archer was known as Pabilsag, known as 'Forefather', and who was said to represent the point at which humans changed from simply being animals to having self-awareness.

Water Mars Pluto

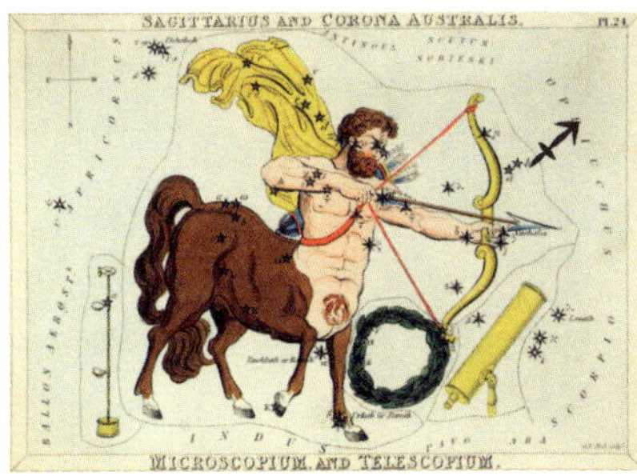

Fire Jupiter

PLANETARY CORRESPONDENCE

Sagittarius's ruling planet is Jupiter, the solar system's biggest planet, symbolizing wise rule, prosperity and generosity. Jupiter is connected to the sephirah of Chesed on the Kabbalistic Tree of Life.

TAROT CORRESPONDENCES

Sagittarius is linked to the card of Temperance, though this card can also be connected to Aquarius, and to the suit of Wands, symbolized by fire.

SYMBOLS

The astrological symbols for November relate to Mars, ♂, and Pluto, ♇, for Scorpio, ♏, as well as to Sagittarius, the Archer, ♐, and the sign's ruler of Jupiter, ♃.

EARTHLY CONNECTIONS

Plants & Trees

REED (*PHRAGMITES AUSTRALIS*)

Esoteric Associations: flexibility and pliancy.

Uses: The reed is a powerful symbol within the Celtic tree calendar, based on fables regarding its strength. The twelfth tree (28 Oct–24 Nov, see page 187), it bends in high winds, remaining flexible, unlike rigid trees, which are prone to topple. Liz Murray, in the *Celtic Tree Oracle*, suggests that it refers to communication (the 8 of Wands in the Tarot, with its flying staffs, has a similar meaning), and sending messages out into the wider world. In some systems, reed, known as *ngetal* in the Ogham alphabet, is connected with broom or fern. As its name suggests, broom is used to make besoms, although these are also made with birch (see page 29). This plant can be invoked for psychic cleansing, just as a broom is used to sweep your house clean.

GINGER (*ZINGIBER OFFICINALE*)

Esoteric Associations: protection, vitality.

Uses: In magical practice, ginger is often used to represent the Fire element, for instance in incenses and oils, and in 'heating up' spells. It is associated with the sign of Scorpio and the planet Mars.

THYME (*THYMUS VULGARIS*)

Esoteric Associations: cleansing, courage, Venus.

Uses: There are indications this was used as a cleanser and purifier in ancient times, and it can be used in the same way today – scatter thyme around a space to purify it.

Gemstones

TOPAZ

Esoteric Associations: protection, strength.

Uses: This November birthstone has different colours, each with different meanings: golden topaz represents the Sun and solar principles such as abundance; blue topaz symbolizes clarity and calmness. Carry whichever colour you most need.

CITRINE

Esoteric Associations: wealth, prosperity.

Uses: Citrine, another November birthstone, is a gemstone of abundance, known as the Merchants' Stone. Carry a piece of citrine to assist in business transactions and commerce.

Runes

HAGALAZ ✦ 28 OCTOBER–13 NOVEMBER

H: Hail. Represents unexpectedness, a sudden stormy period or destruction; a falling apart, new beginnings.

NAUTHIZ ✦ 13–28 NOVEMBER

N: Need. Indicates something you need, but not so much something you want. Has negative connotations.

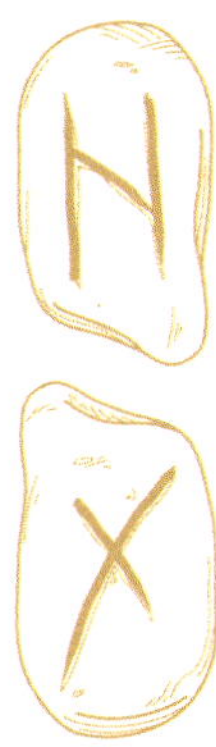

FOLKLORE & MYTH

BONFIRE NIGHT

In the UK, Bonfire Night is held on 5 November to commemorate the failure of Guy Fawkes and his fellow plotters to blow up the English Parliament. Lewes in Sussex also celebrates the Lewes Martyrs, who were burned at the stake in the sixteenth century, for their faith under Queen Mary I. Referred to as the 'biggest bonfire in England', the Lewes Bonfire processions carry seventeen crosses representing the martyrs and feature burning effigies, beating drums, dancing, flaming barrels and torches as well as firework displays.

NOTTE DI ZUCCHERO

The Night of Sugar, held on 2 November in Sicily, is when the dead are said to return and leave children special sweets, such as sugar statues (*Pupi di Zucchero*) and marzipan shaped like fruit (*frutta martorana*). Families go to the graveyard and light candles for their ancestors.

OSIRIS & ISIS MYTH

In the Ancient Egyptian myth, the god Osiris fell victim to a plot by his brother Seth, who had him dismembered. His sister/wife Isis, forced to find his body parts, located all but the god's phallus. It was said that the Nile flooded each year as a result of her tears, shed in grief. After this, he retired to the Underworld to become a lord of the dead. But the war between Osiris and Seth represents the war between fertile land and desert, between the growth of new life and the drying wind (see page 162).

Isis is the Great Queen of the Egyptian pantheon, and in ancient times was worshipped all over the world. She holds the key to the mysteries within the Egyptian tradition and, as the mother of the four canopic jar deities, she is associated with funerary rites. In Dion Fortune's work, *The Sea Priestess*, one of the most haunting portrayals of Isis and regarded as one of the greatest occult novels of the twentieth century, she appears as a goddess of Moon and sea.

Detail of *The Procession of the Lewes Bonfire Boys* by Thomas Henwood, 1853.

XII

DECEMBER

December is the month when many of the great religious festivals, including Christmas and Hanukkah (which sometimes falls in December), are celebrated, as well as the Winter Solstice, or Yule, observed by most contemporary pagans but also by many other traditions across the world. At the darkest point of the year, many spiritual traditions and myths centre on the concept of the light returning and being reborn.

THEMES & ENTITIES

Deities associated with December are linked to time and to a rebirth of the light after the shortest day of the year. This idea is reflected in a myth found in many traditions: the birth of the solar child.

SATURN

An ancient deity, whose name may come from either *satur* – 'stuffed' – or *sator*, a 'sower', Saturn is a god of abundance, of crops and vines. On coins, he carries a sickle or ears of corn. He corresponds to the Greek Cronos, the Babylonian Ninurta and the Hindu god Shani. This huge planet and its accompanying rings were first seen by Galileo in the seventeenth century, but proper identification came later (Galileo couldn't see the rings properly and suggested the planet had ears!).

MITHRAS

The mysteries of Mithras – a Roman deity with Zoroastrian origins – were traditionally celebrated in December; this god of soldiers is also held to have been a divine child born in mid-December. His worship is based on a series of initiatory levels, and Mithraic worshippers today continue to celebrate his birthday.

SKAÐI

This Norse goddess of winter is a patron of skiers, a deity of hunting and is mentioned in the *Poetic Edda*. She is married to Njörðr, a god of the sea, but he dislikes the mountains and she dislikes the coast, so the marriage does not work out. Later, Skaði marries Odin.

HANIEL

ANGELIC CORRESPONDENCE

Haniel, 'Joy of God', is an angel who brings strength and courage, and who encourages family reunion. She is associated with the planet Venus.

KRAMPUS

DEMONIC CORRESPONDENCE

The primary demonic figure associated with December is Krampus, an entity from Alpine folklore. He is a cloven-hoofed, horned devil with a long tongue, who punishes naughty children at Christmas.

SABBATS, FESTIVALS & CELEBRATIONS

December festivals focus on rebirth and the return of the light after the long months of darkness. Spirits rise with the lengthening of days, acknowledging the Unconquered Sun of the soul as well as the cosmological Sun itself.

1 DECEMBER

✳ ***GREATER FEAST FOR DEATH***

A Greater Feast for Death is celebrated on the anniversary of a Thelemite's passing. Aleister Crowley's own death anniversary is observed on 1 December. Thelema does not regard death as the end of life, but as a transition: the words 'A feast for life, and a greater feast for death!' may be uttered during this time. In *The Book of the Law*, Crowley states that the Feast should be 'merry, so as to train people to take the proper view of death'.

10 DECEMBER

○ ✳ ***GANGA-BOIS/GRAND BOIS***

This Haitian vodou festival celebrates the elemental Ganga-Bois, an lwa associated with herbs, plants and trees. With Maître Carrefour (Master Crossroads) and Baron Cimetière (Baron Cemetery), Grand Bois forms a magical triad representing the journey of the soul, from the earth, to the roads on which the soul travels, and finally to the cemetery. Grand Bois is honoured with offerings of honey, herbs and rum.

KEY ○ Historical Event ✳ Annual Event ◇ Variable Dates

17 DECEMBER

SATURNALIA

The Roman festival of the Saturnalia, in honour of the god Saturn, was a 'topsy turvy' seven-day festival of misrule, a period where bay and laurel were brought into the home, and the normal social order was reversed and masters waited on servants. It may also be one of the origins of Yule (see below).

AROUND 21 DECEMBER

WINTER SOLSTICE / YULE

This solstice is a midwinter festival of fire and light, where evergreens are brought into the house and feasts are prepared. To pagans, this is also Yule – the time when the goddess gives birth to a shining son, the Mabon. Modern pagans in the UK gather at dawn at Stonehenge, Newgrange and other ancient sites, many of which were situated to receive the first light of the winter Sun – often heralded as Sol Invictus, the Unconquered Sun.

'I regard as correct the remark of the man who said: "Once December was a month; now it is a year."'

—Seneca, on Saturnalia preparations

20 OR 24 DECEMBER

MODRANIHT

Also known as Mothers' Night, this Anglo-Saxon festival is celebrated on the night before 25 December or, more usual today, on the night of 20 December before the Solstice itself. It is still celebrated today by followers of Norse paganism as the first of the twelve days of Yule. Practitioners may hold a feast, light candles and honour the female ancestors, known as the Disir.

RITUALS, SPELLS & DIVINATION

WINTER SOLSTICE RITUAL

Decorate your altar or special place with mistletoe, holly leaves and berries, and other seasonal decorations. Set up your ritual as you are accustomed, calling the quarters and purifying with water and fire (see page 189).

You may wish to work with the Holly King and the Oak King, visualizing their ritual battle (see page 92). Or choose to honour the goddess in her role as the Lady who gives birth to the sacred child, the Mabon. Light a white candle for the goddess, symbolizing the Sun's return, and make an offering of honey or mead. Or work with the Sun itself – rise at dawn on the morning of the Winter Solstice at a sacred site or somewhere near you, and watch the Sun rise above the horizon.

For this, you will need:

- One red candle
- One green candle
- One white candle
- Water and incense (make this using myrrh, frankincense and pine resin)

TAROT

The Winter Solstice or New Year's Eve (see page 22) are good times to undertake Tarot readings for the six months ahead. Take particular note of any Major Arcana cards that appear in your reading at this numinous time (see page 188).

NUMEROLOGY

December is associated numerologically with 3, linking to Jupiter, the ruler of Sagittarius, and representing sincerity and spiritual understanding.

'December is the month the old grief ends, and the new year lays the path with new happiness.'

—Russian saying

Stonehenge by Henry Mark Anthony (1817–1886).

CELESTIAL MAGIC

In December, Fire solidifies into Earth as the zodiac shifts, and the nights are at their longest before the return of the Sun at the Winter Solstice. The winter constellations – Orion, the Bull and the Pleiades among them – are at their brightest in the cold winter skies.

MOONS

December's Full Moon is known as the Cold Moon or Long Nights Moon in Nordic custom and among the Oneida and Mahican peoples of North America.

METEOR SKIES

The Geminids occur around 13–14 December, with the Ursids occurring just after the Solstice on 22 December.

In December, Jupiter and Saturn appear relatively close to each other and the Moon, with the Moon passing by them. The famous 2020 'Great Conjunction' saw them extremely close (0.1 degrees apart).

ELEMENTAL & ZODIAC CORRESPONDENCES

In December, the zodiac shifts and deepens from the element of Fire and Sagittarius the Archer, into the element of Earth and Capricorn.

PLANETARY CORRESPONDENCES

This month's planets are Jupiter and Saturn. Together, when they appear in the so-called 'Great Conjunction,' which can occur in December, they may be seen as a single, immensely bright star – some claim it is the star that led the Three Kings to the stable at Bethlehem. In Kabbalistic terms, Saturn – Capricorn's ruler – is related to Binah ('the great sea'), which represents understanding and is the highest female aspect of the universe. It contains the energy of endings and beginnings and is a good place to go if you are seeking answers to questions that have been obscure.

TAROT CORRESPONDENCES

In the Tarot, December is sometimes linked to The Star, a spiritual card of balance and hope, although it is also connected to The Devil (Capricorn) and Temperance (Sagittarius).

SYMBOLS

December's astrological symbols are Sagittarius, ♐, ruled by Jupiter, ♃, and Saturn, ♄, the ruler of Capricorn, ♑.

EARTHLY CONNECTIONS

Plants & Trees

ELDER (*SAMBUCAS NIGER*)

Esoteric Associations: witchcraft, magic, protection.

Uses: Elder is the thirteenth tree in the Celtic tree calendar (25 Nov–22 Dec, see page 187). The name comes from the Saxon *ellaern* (hollow) or *aeld* (fire), possibly because its hollow twigs were used to blow life into fires. Planting elder near your home is said to offer protection, and to attract fairies (see page 185).

MISTLETOE (*VISCUM ALBUM*)

Esoteric Associations: fertility, immortality and rebirth.

Uses: A familiar part of Christmas and Solstice decorations today, mistletoe is one of the evergreens brought into the house at this time of year. Its use today is magical rather than medicinal, as the berries are highly poisonous, although a derivative of mistletoe is used in anti-cancer treatments. It appears in Greek mythology and also in Norse legend – the god Balder was killed by a dart made out of mistletoe. **Toxic: do not ingest.**

CINNAMON (*CINNAMOMUM VERUM*)

Esoteric Associations: protection, attracting prosperity.

Uses: This warming, spicy plant is an ideal ingredient to use as part of a winter incense (see page 165).

BLACKTHORN (*PRUNUS SPINOSA*)

Esoteric Associations: protection, transition, banishing negativity.

Uses: Blackthorn is associated with the darker half of the year in Celtic lore. Its thorns are used in protective charms and banishing spells; it is regarded as a purgative.

Gemstones

TURQUOISE

Esoteric Associations: healing, new beginnings.

Uses: A December birthstone, turquoise is a stone of healing, and said to promote creativity and spiritual growth.

TANZANITE

Esoteric Associations: calm, soothing, transformation.

Uses: Also a December birthstone, tanzanite is said to promote psychic awareness and inner calm.

ZIRCON

Esoteric Associations: healing, protective energy.

Uses: This December birthstone is said in folklore to ward off evil and promote healing and calm.

Runes

ISA ✦ 28 NOVEMBER–13 DECEMBER

I: Ice. A challenge or frustration, Isa inhibits and constricts but also has the quality of preservation.

JERA ✦ 13–28 DECEMBER

J or Y: A year, a good harvest. A rune of prosperity and fulfilment. Nurture planted seeds, to gain their fruits.

Yule cat

FOLKLORE & MYTH

SHOE THROWING

In Czechia, at Christmas, women stand with their backs to the front door and throw shoes over their shoulders to divine their marital prospects in the coming year. Those prospects are good if a shoe lands with its toe facing towards the door.

YALDA NIGHT

Shabe Yalda is an ancient Persian Winter Solstice festival, still celebrated by some in Afghanistan. People stay up late, eat pomegranates, and the oldest member of the household tells stories.

POOR OLD HOSS

Similar to the Mari Lwyd (see page 30), the Poor Old Hoss is a black-robed figure topped with a horse skull. It is joined by a troupe of hunters with holly-decked hats who parade around Richmond, Yorkshire, UK, in December.

MUMMERS' PLAYS

Held in December in the British Isles and dating from medieval times, these feature stylized battles between good and evil, often with St George and the Dragon.

THE YULE CAT

This gigantic supernatural cat in Icelandic folklore pounces on people who do not receive new clothes for Christmas.

HIDING BROOMS

In Norway, people hide brooms and mops in December, so that they might not be used by witches or other evil spirits.

ELDER LEGENDS

Elder is known as the witch's tree (a witch was thought to be able to turn into one), and witches were said to wear crowns of elder stems, or withies, at Samhain. You must apologize to elder if you cut it. In Denmark the Elder Mother will haunt wood taken from this tree without her permission – a tradition found across England, too. In Ireland, making a cradle from elder is said to be dangerous, as the fairies will steal a child placed in it. If you take the back of the green bark of elder, apply it to your skin at Samhain and then stand near a fairy hill, it is believed that you may see a fairy procession go by!

DIVINATION DIRECTORY

PRACTICAL KABBALAH: Also known as the Cabbala, Kabbala or Qabbala, which derives from the Hebrew word, 'to receive'. This ancient system of mysticism originates in Judaism and was taken up by later occultists, such as Eliphas Levi, who synthesized elements of Judaic Kabbalism with the Tarot, alchemy and Hermetic principles (Hermeticism is a philosophical or religious tradition with occult associations). The occult version of Kabbalism is based around the Tree of Life: this is a map of the planets and the realms beyond, known as the sephiroth. The Tree is said to be an emanation from the mind of God, becoming increasingly material as we go down the Tree, and not really accessible to human understanding at its higher reaches. Earth lies at the bottom, in the sphere, or sephirah, known as Malkuth. The sephiroth can be used as meditational or visualization tools, operating as a 'mind map' to explore the psyche. You will find Kabbalistic pathworking in the 'Rituals, Spells & Divinations' sections as well as correspondences in the 'Celestial Magic' sections.

The sephiroth are arranged in three pillars: (A) Mercy (right), (B) Severity (left) and (C) Equilibrium (centre).

Its ten spheres (sephiroth) are:
(1) Keter כתר (Crown, the Divine)
(2) Chokmah חכמה (Wisdom)
(3) Binah בינה (Understanding, the Great Sea, Structure, Discipline, Feminine)
(4) Chesed חסד (Kindness, Mercy)
(5) Gevurah גבורה (Severity, Justice, Vigour, Might, Masculinity)
(6) Tiphareth תפארת (Beauty, Harmony, Sun)
(7) Netzach נצח (Victory, Endurance, Love, Intuition, Femininity)
(8) Hod הוד (Splendour, Majesty, Intellect)
(9) Yesod יסוד (Foundation, Moon, Psychic)
(10) Malkuth מלכות (Kingdom, Kingship).

Right: The Tree of Life, with its three pillars and ten spheres or sephiroth.

CELTIC TREE CALENDAR: This is based on the Irish Ogham alphabet, which has been found mainly on stones throughout the ancient Celtic world. It is said to have been devised by Ogma, the god of writing, though may have been derived from Norse runes (see right), or from Greek writing, as there were connections between Ancient Greece and the Celtic world (the Greek word for writing is *ogmos*). In modern times, it has become linked with a system of correspondences that loosely connects thirteen trees to the months of the year, each with different meanings derived from the folklore of Britain and Ireland. As with the zodiac, you can have a birth tree. The ancient Celts themselves almost certainly had a different system (likely to be lunar) and this modern equivalent derives ultimately from the work of writer Robert Graves. The 'Earthly Connections' sections often highlight trees from this calendar.

RUNES: There are several variations on this Northern European system of divination, including the Elder Futhark (150 BCE–800 CE), the Old English Futhorc (400–1100 CE) and the Younger Futhark (800–1100 CE). The Elder Futhark divides into three sets of eight, known as the *aettir* (each set is an *aett*). As an alphabet, it was replaced by the Roman letters around 700 CE but continued as a decorative system. There is not a lot of evidence that they were originally used for divination, but they were intended for inscriptions and perhaps as magical charms. The 'Earthly Connections' sections highlight which two runes from the Elder Futhark are relevant for each month, along with their associations – these are often known as 'birth runes' in a similar manner to birthstones or zodiac signs. In the part-saga known as the *Hávamál*, Odin credits runes with being able to restore the dead to life.

Right: The Celtic tree calendar partitions the year into thirteen trees, bar 23 December, which is not ruled by any tree but is sometimes thought to be represented by mistletoe. Known as 'the Nameless Day', it was considered by the Druids to be outside the realm of time.

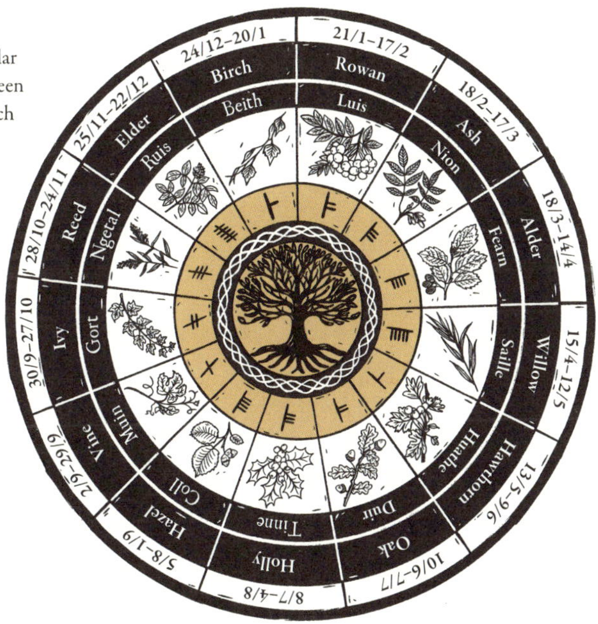

THELEMA / ALEISTER CROWLEY: Born 12 October, 1875 in Leamington Spa, UK, Aleister Crowley was a member of the Golden Dawn, a secret society that was hugely influential in later occult and magical practices such as Wicca. He wrote several works on the occult, including *The Book of the Law*, which is used in many rites and celebrations listed in this book. After a mystical experience in Egypt in the early 1900s, Crowley founded the magical system known as Thelema, a religious movement inspired by Ancient Egyptian gods and beliefs. From him comes the quote, 'Do what thou wilt shall be the whole of the Law', followed by 'Love is the Law; love under will'.

TAROT: The Tarot is one of Western Europe's oldest and most respected divinatory systems. It consists of seventy-eight illustrated playing cards used for divination and guidance. Its origins remain unclear, but the Tarot may have been devised as a form of flattering accessory to the Visconti family of Milan in the fifteenth century. In this early stage, the cards were a game – known as *tarocchi*. One of today's most common decks is the Rider Waite – the illustrations (by Pixie Colman Smith) are used in this book.

A Tarot deck consists of two types of cards: the twenty-two Major Arcana (*arcana* means 'secrets') and the fifty-six Minor Arcana. The Major Arcana follow an apocryphal journey through life and are numbered 0 to 21. The Major Arcana include: 0 The Fool; 1 The Magician; 2 The High Priestess; 3 The Empress; 4 The Emperor; 5 The Hierophant; 6 The Lovers; 7 The Chariot; 8 Strength; 9 The Hermit; 10 Wheel of Fortune; 11 Justice; 12 The Hanged Man; 13 Death; 14 Temperance; 15 The Devil; 16 The Tower; 17 The Star; 18 The Moon; 19 The Sun; 20 Judgement; 21 The World.

We begin with the Fool (0), who blithely steps from a cliff. Following his descent, the Fool passes through a series of meetings with archetypal figures – the Empress, the High Priestess, the Hermit, Death and the Sun and Moon among others – journeying into the hinterlands of the Underworld before rising back up again in the Day of Judgement and becoming reborn into the World. The Major Arcana are the 'big cards', indicating major influences when they turn up in a reading.

The Minor Arcana's fifty-six cards run parallel to the suits of the playing card deck: Swords (diamonds); Wands (clubs); Cups (hearts); Pentacles (spades), with each suit numbered from 1 to 10, along with four 'figure' cards: The Page; The Knight; The Queen; and The King.

Above: The Fool (0) and The World (21) cards from the Rider–Waite Tarot.

Each suit's general associations are as follows:
Swords: east, air, morning, the intellect.
Wands: south, fire, noon, passion, motivation.
Cups: west, water, evening, the emotions.
Pentacles: north, earth, midnight, practical matters.

Tarot correspondences and divination practices or readings for the month can be found in the 'Celestial Magic' and 'Rituals, Spells & Divination' sections.

NUMEROLOGY: This system of mystical numbers is based on the premise that each number has a particular energy and set of correspondences. Many societies and cultures follow their own systems of numerology, such as the Ancient Greek, Chinese, Tamil or Chaldean systems.

To find your personal number, write out your entire birthdate (including the full year) and add each individual number. For example, **14021972** = **26**. Then add '**2**' and '**6**' and you get **8**, which will be your life path number to represent your destiny, your personality traits and general path in life. Each month's numerological associations can be found in 'Rituals, Spells & Divination' sections.

ANGELS & DEMONS: These appear throughout the history of Western magic, and many grimoires focus on demonic conjuration, in which the magician summons a demon to accomplish a particular purpose, such as gaining wealth. The grimoire *The Lesser Key of Solomon*, for instance, features a range of seventy-two demons and explains the art of goetia, from the Greek *goēteia* ('sorcery' or 'charms'); the art of summoning demons. The angelic realm, however, is more powerful, and angels have power over demons.

ALTAR: An altar is used for spellwork, rituals and intentions, and can be placed on any solid surface. Covered with an appropriate cloth, it should contain:

- A cup or chalice
- An athame (ritual knife)
- A wand
- An incense holder
- A dish of earth, or a stone or crystal

DIVINATION: The book's 'Rituals, Spells & Divination' sections offer divination techniques, from scrying (glimpsing the future in a bowl of ink or water) and Kabbalistic pathworking to performing Tarot spreads or casting runes. There are many resources both in books and on the internet if you feel drawn to any particular system.

DRAWING A CIRCLE: Some rituals and spells in this book begin with casting or drawing a circle. We do so to separate our ritual space from the everyday world and denote it as sacred. Begin facing east and then 'draw' a circle in the air, around head height, using a wand or athame (ritual knife). Do so sunwise: east, south, west, north and then return to the east. To take the circle down, do the same thing widdershins (east, north, west, south), imagining the energy of the circle passing back through the wand or athame back to the earth.

CLEANSING: To cleanse a space of negative energies and focus intention, light a smudge stick made of sage or other herbs and waft it, starting in the east. You can also place crystals on windowsills to purify your space.

FIRE: Fire releases spellwork into the universe, burning affirmations or intentions written on paper. **Be extremely careful to do so safely, ideally using a fire-proof container.**

INDEX

PICTURE CREDITS & ACKNOWLEDGEMENTS

T = top, B = bottom, L = left, C = centre, R = right

The publisher would like to thank the following for the permission to reproduce copyright material.

Alamy: 9 Granger–Historical Picture Archive; 18 Interfoto; 20BR Reading Room 2020; 32 Interfoto; 34BL Chronicle; 39 (botanicals) Marcus Harrison; 44 Artepics; 46 Interfoto; 48BL Interfoto; 49T Artokoloro/ Penta Springs Limited; 53 Artefact; 60 Interfoto; 66 Realy Easy Star; 73 Granger –Historical Picture Archive; 76BL Art Collection; 88 Interfoto; 91TL Granger–Historical Picture Archive; 100 Painters; 102 Interfoto; 104B piemags:rmn; 116 Interfoto; 130 Interfoto; 133TR CPA Media Pte Ltd. (main image); 137 Peter Horree; 144 Interfoto; 150 Painters; 158 Interfoto; 161CR Granger–Historical Picture Archive; 171 Artgen; 174 Interfoto; 175 Walker Art Library; 183T ilbusca.

Getty Images: 7 Fine Art Images/Heritage Images; 11, 124, 180 (stars) ilbusca; 15 Dirty Fellas; 21CL Credit Prisma/UniversalImagesGroup; 25 Historical Picture Archive; 27CR Science & Society Picture Library; 27TR, 181TR Science & Society Picture Library; 29, 43, 57, 71, 85, 99, 113, 127, 141, 155, 169, 183, 189BR (runes) samposnick; 54, 82, 110, 166, 180 (stars) Universal History Archive/Universal Images Group; 54BC Credit Universal History Archive/Universal Images Group; 54 duncan1890; 55TR/C Science & Society Picture Library; 62BR Bettman; 66 Photo by © Historical Picture Archive/Corbis; 69T Science & Society Picture Library; 73 Bettmann; 80 Bettmann; 81 duncan 1890; 90TL (main image) Nastasic; 95 bauhaus1000; 97T Science & Society Picture Library; 105CL ilbusca; 105TR duncan1890; 110 duncan1890 (moon); 112C mikroman6; 115 Heritage Images; 119TL/CR Nastasic; 122 Heritage Images; 124 mikroman6 (meteor); 125T/C Credit Science & Society Picture Library; 126C ilbusca; 129 Nastasic; 132TR bauhaus1000; 132BL powerofforever; 133T/C Heritage Image; 146 Ivy Close Images; 153T Science & Society Picture Library; 160BL Grafissimo; 174BL duncan1890; 179 WAVE The Museums, Galleries and Archives of Wolverhampton; 180 ibusca (starburst) 180 mikroman6 (Saturn/Jupiter).

Shutterstock: 10TR Morphart Creation; 10BL robin.ph; 9, 27, 55, 69, 97, 125, 153, 181, 188 (Tarot cards) Roman Sibiryakov; 11, 20, 76, 77, 86, 90, 91, 105, 132, 133, 160, 175, 186 (frame) Kakaldey6996; 12–13B Media Guru; 20TL juliawhite; 27, 41, 51, 55, 69, 83. 97, 111, 125, 139, 153, 167, 181 (zodiac signs) Olga Lobko; 27, 55, 69, 97, 125, 153, 181 (frame) Thrifty Tracker; 28 From top Suwi19, dutko_vika, Epine, Foxyliam; 29T vector_ann; 39 Kseniakron; 41TL/CL Rawpixel.com; 42T B. illustrations, 42C Aniok, 42B mart; 43T FarbaKolerova, 43C Kseniakrop; 56T Bodor Tivadar; 56C Channarong Pherngjanda; 56B Morphart Creation; 57T Channarong Pherngjanda; 62TL Morphart Creation; 63CL Sry85; 70T Weredragon; 70C greenga; 70B Feodora_21; 71T Nina Images; 83TL/CL Rawpixel.com; 84T Elena Skugar; 84B Modesta.Gas; 85T Bodor Tivadar; 85C logaryphmic; 97C Lina Keil (C); 98T Yevheniia Lytvynovych; 98B Foxyliam; 99T Channarong Pherngjanda; 108 vda_82 (surround); Salomi art (star); 111TR/BR Credit Rawpixel.com; 112T Rina Osh; 112B Morphart Creation; 113T Alexander_P; 126C jottaonni; 126B indigo.arty; 127 Masha_tolk_art; 139TL/CL Rawpixel.com; 140T Artverza; 140B Epine; 140TR daniela_designs; 154T Farba Kolerova; 154C Sabelskaia; 154B Yevheniia Lytvynovych; 155T Yevheniia Lytvynovych; 160TR Morphant Creations; 164 KO-SIM; 166 Vlada Young (moon face); 166 Natalia Mikhalchuk (clouds); 167TR/ CR Rawpixel.com; 168T Bodor Tivadar; 168B Arthur Balitskii; 169T Alisles; 174TR Sektor Creative Design; 180BL Media Guru (moon surface); 182T Art tori; 182C Bodor Tivadar; 182B EngravingFactory; 186 Sidhe.

Wellcome Collection: 11 The microcosm (man) and the macrocosm (the world). Line engraving by T. de Bry, 1617.

Wikimedia: 26, 96, 124, 152 (constellations) NYPL via internet Archive/archive.org; 48TR internet Archive/ archive.org; 77TR Saskia Jansen personal collection/1909 Roses & Lilies Waite-Smith Tarot deck; 186 AnonMoos.

Illustrations: 15, 21TL BR, 31, 34TR, 35TL CR BL, 40, 49CL BR, 58, 63TR, 68, 76TR, 77CL BR, 87, 90BR, 91CR BL, 104TL, 105BR, 118BL TR, 119BL, 133BL, 138, 142, 147TL CR BL, 157, 161TL BL, 166, 175TR BR, 184, 187 Daisy Webster; 27, 41, 55, 69, 83, 97, 111, 125, 139, 153, 167, 181 (symbols) Jane Lanaway.

AUTHOR ACKNOWLEDGEMENTS

A huge thank you to Laura Anstey, Sef Salem, Trevor Jones and Veronica Williams, for all their support in the last year. And thank you, too, to Ronald, Ana, Liz, Penny, Adrian, Su and JJ.